Blessed
Be Our
TABLE

6/2/05

With birthday greetings
& love.

Viv and David

Graces for mealtimes & reflections on food

Blessed Be Our TABLE

Neil Paynter

WILD GOOSE PUBLICATIONS

www.ionabooks.com

Compilation © 2003 Neil Paynter
Prayers and readings © the individual contributors
First published 2003 by
Wild Goose Publications, Fourth Floor, Savoy House,
140 Sauchiehall Street, Glasgow G2 3DH, UK,
the publishing division of the Iona Community. Scottish Charity No. SCO03794.
Limited Company Reg. No. SCO96243.

ISBN 1 901557 72 3

Cover design © 2002 Wild Goose Publications
Cover painting by Delia Cavers, www.DeliaCavers.co.uk
Cover painting and design © Wild Goose Publications

Neil Paynter has asserted his right in accordance with the Copyright, Designs and
Patents Act, 1988, to be identified as the author of this compilation and the individual
contributors have asserted their right to be identified as authors of their contributions.

A catalogue record for this book is available from the British Library.

Overseas distribution
Australia: Willow Connection Pty Ltd, Unit 4A, 3-9 Kenneth Road, Manly Vale, NSW 2093
New Zealand: Pleroma, Higginson Street, Otane 4170, Central Hawkes Bay
Canada: Novalis Publishing & Distribution, 49 Front Street East, Toronto, Ontario M5E 1B3

Permission to reproduce any part of this work in Australia
or New Zealand should be sought from Willow Connection.

Printed by Bell & Bain, Thornliebank, Glasgow

For everyone who has worked in the Iona Abbey
and MacLeod Centre kitchens
For my family
For friends who have fed me

Thank you

The title of this book, *Blessed Be Our Table*, is inspired by the final line of 'A grace for eating alone' by Nicola Slee (p66).

CONTENTS

Daily worship together will be the essence of our witness, and our common meals together will serve to remind us that the Table of the Lord is not something that must happen 'quarterly' but must happen daily, if really the Common Life is to be won again for God.

~ *George MacLeod*

INTRODUCTION

Food is the basic material of life. It is essential for survival. How easy it is for those of us who live in comfort to take it for granted; not even think about it; unwrap the packaging; consume the sanitised product. We are far removed from its source and origin: from the Creator, from the Earth, from those who tend and produce it – and from the injustice and hunger that is the daily reality of many of the folk who provide food for our tables.

I live and work in rural Cumbria where farmers have suffered much in recent years from unrealistically low prices, driven down by the power of supermarkets and the demand for cheap food, bringing many to the brink of bankruptcy and despair. The same story can be told all over the upland fringes of Britain. And the same story can be told, too, for farmers in the world's poorer countries. The causes of injustice there are very similar: the power of large companies to drive prices down, an unfair system of trade controlled by the powerful, unequal land distribution, our constant desire for cheaper and cheaper food. But the consequences for the food producers and their families in poor countries are even more stark: disease and death, migration and starvation.

We need to make these links.

Here at Stillicidia, our Christian house of welcome, we see saying grace before our meals as a vital part of this reconnection. It gives us pause before we eat to express our thankfulness to God, and to remember where our food has come from.

This book of graces is so valuable because it integrates thankfulness with a burning passion for justice, both of which are central to our relationship with a bountiful provider God, with the whole wondrous creation, with each other, and with our sisters and brothers throughout the world who, because of greed and injustice, will not receive their daily bread today.

The joy of this book is that we are invited to pray, and recommit ourselves to act for justice each time we join in the simple sharing of a meal. It is also very much a celebration – of food, of diversity, of community and sharing, of Creator and creation. So, come let us celebrate!

~ *Helen Boothroyd*

Helen Boothroyd works as social responsibility administrator for Churches Together in Cumbria. She is a Trustee of Carlisle One World Centre, which aims to raise awareness and promote action to address the causes of poverty and injustice, and a member of the local ecumenical justice and peace group, currently involved in campaigning to promote and link fair trade and local trade. She and her husband run Stillicidia, a Christian house of welcome.

Washing one's hands

Luke 11:37–42

Washing one's hands of the conflict between the powerful and the powerless means to side with the powerful, not to be neutral.

~ *Paulo Freire, CAFOD*

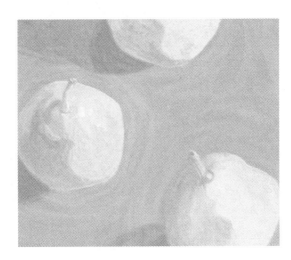

For the
HANDS

From the hand of God

In our artificial technological society, we have inserted so many secondary causes between ourselves and the great first cause, that we are apt to leave God out of our reckoning altogether. We don't think of our bread as coming from the hand of God ... There are some simple lines of poetry that go like this:

Back of the loaf is the snowy flour;
back of the flour is the mill;
and back of the mill is the sun and shower,
and the wheat and the Father's will.

(Traditional miller's grace, source unknown)

~ The Very Rev. Dr George Reid

A flame of love

Each thing we have received,
from you it came, O God.
Each thing for which we hope,
from your love it will be given.
Kindle in our hearts within
a flame of love to our neighbours,
to our foes, to our friends, to our loved ones all,
from the lowliest thing that lives,
to the name that is highest of all.
Amen.

~ Gaelic traditional

A prayer in Zulu

Mdali siyakubonga ngothando lwakho
nangesineke sakho nezipho osipha zona
ngiyakudumisa ngalokho. Amen

Creator, we thank you for your love,
your patience, and the gifts you give us.
We thank you for this food. Amen

~ Peter Mhlophe, Mamelodi, near Pretoria, South Africa

You have poured your gifts

O Lord, once again you have poured your gifts on us with
undeserved generosity. Accept our humble and thankful praise.

~ Stella Durand

From thy bounty

Bless us, O Lord, and these gifts we are about to receive from thy bounty.
Through Christ our Lord.
Amen

(Traditional Catholic grace before meals)

~ From Dom Aidan Murray, OSB, the Worth Abbey Lay Community

All things come from you

All things come from you, O Lord. Once more you gift us
with plenty. Help us to share what you have given.

~ Stella Durand

Couscous

Good God!

As I love the hands that made this food
more than food itself
so feed me love
for hands
that made the hands
and bless my life with health. Amen

~ David Coleman
(NB I am not very keen on couscous!)

Grace

I handle this bowl with respect
I lift this cup with reverence
I wipe this plate with thankfulness
I receive this food with gratitude

From you, mother earth
From you, brother human
From you, father time
From you, sister sustenance

I worship

~ *Nicola Slee*

Food from the world

Snug in blankets, made of Australian wool,
in cotton from Egypt, on Scandinavian timber
we slept; and wakened to find food from the world
on our table. Marvellous! Amen

~ *Ian M. Fraser*

For the food on this table

Thanks be to God for the food on this table.
Bless those who grew it, caught it, transported it;
bless those who prepared it, sold it, cooked it;
and thanks be to God that we can eat it.

~ *Chris Polhill*

Grace

For
the farmers and the fishers
the gatherers and growers
the cooks and caterers
we give You thanks.

~ Alix Brown

God bless the backs that ache

God bless the backs that ache from working in the fields.
God bless the hands that smart from labouring in the factories.
God bless the fingers that burn from cooking over the fire.
God bless our bodies that will consume the sacrifice of others' lives.

~ Nicola Slee

For all the work

For all the work that brings this food to our table;
for cook and shopkeeper,
for field-worker and shipping agent,
for merchant and shop assistant,
and for our own God-given ability to work and earn,
we give thanks. Amen

~ Donald Hilton

Behind the soil

Behind the soil, the creator
behind the grain, the researcher
behind the harvest, the weather, the manufacturer
behind the spread table, the cooking and baking:
We thank God for gifts given direct and through others
Amen

~ *Ian M. Fraser*

For the candle

For the candle that gives its light
for the rose that proffers its perfume
for the hands that offer their labour
for the friends who share their fellowship
for the food that makes our sustenance
thanks be to God.

~ *Nicola Slee*

For the good earth

For the good earth, Lord God; for those who make it productive;
for those who cook and bake and serve: we give thanks. Amen

~ *Ian M. Fraser*

May we remember

Lord, as we eat,
may we remember those who
grew,
harvested,
carried,
sold,
chose,
cooked,
and served this food;
and let us be mindful of our debt to them, and to You.
Amen

~ Jane Bentley

The hand that made the hands

For the hands that tilled,
for the hands that harvested,
for the hands that processed,
for the hands that transported,
for the hands that stocked,
for the hands that sold,
for the hands that bought,
for the hands that prepared,
for the hands that will hold,
for the hand that made the hands,
our hearts are forever grateful.
Amen

~ Ewan Aitken

For those known and unknown

For those we know who prepared this food
out of love and kindness,
we give thanks.
For those unknown
who worked to earn
and earned to live,
and by their living serve us now,
we give thanks. Amen

~ *Donald Hilton*

May they be blessed

Whoever plucked these fruits,
    may they be blessed.
Whoever sorted and cleaned, packaged and prepared these foods,
    may they be blessed.
Whoever dreamed the recipes, concocted the flavours, experimented with
   the mixtures,
    may they be blessed.
Whoever chopped or mashed, sautéed or puréed; whipped, beat or folded;
   fried, baked or poached,
     may they be blessed.
And whoever eats, with appetite large or small, body young or old,
    may we, too, be blessed.

~ *Nicola Slee*

Grace

Farmers
and fishers
lorry drivers
and shopkeepers
cooks
and washers up.
God bless them
God bless us
God bless our food.

~ Ruth Burgess

Thank you

Thank you, heavenly Father,
for people who prepare meals each day.
Thank you for cooks and those who wash up.
Thank you for those who serve tea and coffee.
In Jesus' name. Amen

~ Richard Bowers

A blessing on this food

A blessing on this food
and all who have prepared it.
A blessing on this house

and all who eat within it.
A blessing on the work
of buying and selling,
of carrying and storing,
of farming and of harvesting.
A blessing on the land and all who live upon it.
A blessing on the rain and sun,
the care of the Creator.
A blessing on this food.
Amen

~ Brian Woodcock

LINKED TOGETHER

Jesus confronted and confronts the monopoly of power: raising women, sick people, people of no apparent significance, to stand tall and be subjects of their own lives as individuals and communities; to refuse, wherever they are, to be labelled as 'underdeveloped' or an 'underclass'. That's what food co-ops, credit unions on our housing estates and rural development groups … such as the Society for Integrated Rural Development in South India can do. That's what imaginative trading can do when goods are linked with people and their needs; when labour is energy not a commodity. Just imagine what could happen if all such small groups throughout the world linked together to try to resist imaginatively the dominance of economics over human need.

~ Joy Mead

Some prayers for the food chain

1

Lord, we pray for all those who have helped
bring this food to our table. Help us to remember
that what we choose to eat and drink
makes a difference to the lives of others.

2

For food and fellowship and for all things
fairly traded, dear Lord, we give thanks.

3

Lord, this food unites us with farmers, suppliers,
shoppers and cooks. Thank you for all who
have played a part in bringing food to this table.

4

Remembering those who grew
and those who gathered,
those who shipped and those who shopped,
those who cooked and those who served,
for all these things, dear Lord, we give thanks.

~ Fiona Ritchie Walker/Traidcraft

People far away

Dear God,
We know that the food that we eat and drink
is grown by people far away.
Even though we will never meet them,
help us to care for their needs as well as our own.

~ Christian Aid

A fair trade

God, thank you for:

fresh herbs and
exotic spices

local produce and
tropical fruit

for the bounty and gifts of your good earth.

May we remember all who work the land.
May our choices and actions be seeds that grow
to yield our sisters and brothers a rich harvest
of healthier working conditions, living wages,
a fair trade ...
Amen

~ Neil Paynter

God of the just weight

God of the just weight
and the fair measure,
let me remember the hands
that harvested my food, my drink,
not only in my prayers
but in the marketplace.
Let me not seek a bargain
that leaves others hungry.

~ Christian Aid/Janet Morley

Praise be to you

Praise be to you, O Lord,
who has nourished us from our youth onwards:
give food to all living creatures,
and fill our hearts with joy and gladness,
through Christ, our Lord. Amen

~ from Syria, 4th century

Readings:

Psalm 19:1
Psalm 104:27–28
Psalm 138:8
Psalm 145:16
Isaiah 64:8
Isaiah 66:2
Acts 7:49–50

Our daily
BREAD

On breaking bread

This is not an attempt to get around Eucharist problems! It is exactly what it says. We use it as a couple any time we really are breaking open a new loaf, or, more often than not, sharing a plate of rolls, having a sandwich picnic or even in a cafe. I have set it out as we use it for two voices. I will outline at the end variations that have been used by our families or guests.

Participants lay a hand on or over the bread

Voice 1: 'They knew Him in the breaking of Bread ...'

Voice 2: In the renewing of the Covenant made by God with the whole human race.

Voice 1: May we now know Him as we renew our Covenant with each other.

Voice 2: And with all whose lives touch ours.

Together: Deep peace (*the bread is broken*). Shalom (*the bread is shared*).

Variations:
   a) Voice 1 as given, with all guests doing Voice 2.
   b) When four persons present, all take a voice each. Or go two by two.
   c) Divide voices male/female – good when children are present.
   d) At line four, all say this, then instead of all saying line five together, say 'Deep peace' to each person as the bread is passed around the table, and conclude with 'Shalom' said together.

We have found the last variation good if there are a lot of guests and some are a bit lost, especially children who have not got the hang of all the words but can join in the last bit and enjoy passing the plate as well, if that is what you are doing.

~ Maire-Colette Wilkie

Real bread

A twelve-year-old staying in the MacLeod Centre was offered a slice of whole-meal bread freshly baked in the Centre's kitchen. The child didn't accept the bread and asked, 'Can I have some real bread?' How many of us have heard a child say something like this? For many children, real bread comes wrapped in plastic, and is white and pre-sliced ...

Creator God, thank you for good wholesome grain
free of pollution, residues of pesticides, and
manipulation by geneticists.

Thank you for good wholesome flour,
unbleached by toxic substances, and milled in a way
which retains all the nutrients with which you blessed it.

Thank you for freshly baked bread,
made in kitchens and local bakeries, filling our homes and neighbourhoods
with the most beautiful, heavenly-earthy smell.

Creator God, thank you for real grain, to provide real flour,
to make real bread.
Living bread Jesus blessed and broke and shared.

~ John Harrison and Neil Paynter
  (adapted from an evening liturgy, Iona Abbey)

Bread in our hands

Bread in our hands
Thankfulness in our hearts
Bless you God

~ Ruth Burgess

God who clothes the meadows

God who clothes the meadows (or machair)
with colour of flowers,
who gives birds of the air their food,
we thank you that we have bread today
and know that we need not fear tomorrow.

~ Jan Sutch Pickard

Grace

God who made the sun and rain
God who cheered the growing grain
God who gives us daily bread
Bless us now as we are fed.

~ Ruth Burgess

He broke bread

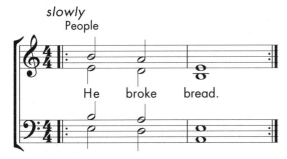

slowly
People

He   broke   bread.

Repeat this chant many times
whilst verses are spoken.

Soloists

Soloists sing their chant with the People's
chant joining after the first chant has been
sung a number of times.

He   broke   bread.

1. He broke bread
   there were very many
   and they were hungry.

2. He broke bread
   with his closest friends
   at a meal.

3. He broke bread
   after walking with them
   and he was gone.

4. He said he was the bread
   sent by the Father.

5. So we are full.
   We break bread together
   to follow his example
   and be changed.

*Verses to be read whilst chant is sung,
leaving gaps between each verse to
relect and listen to the chant.*

~ *Text & music: Pat Livingstone, Oran*

Sharing our bread

For I received from the Lord the teaching that I passed on to you:
that the Lord Jesus, on the night he was betrayed, took a piece of bread, gave
thanks to God, broke it, and said 'This is my body, which is for you.
Do this in memory of me.' (1 Cor. 11:23–24)

'The great community problem of our modern world is how to share bread.'

These words were said by George MacLeod, the Founder of the Iona Community, several decades ago. They are no less true now than they were then. More so, for we know that the gap between the rich of the earth, among whom we must count ourselves, and the earth's poor, after thirty post-war years of narrowing, has been followed by twenty years in which it has got wider – so wide that there has never been a time in human history when it was so great, or affected so many people. Truly, Lazarus is far away …

Bread, of course, as well as being real, also stands as a symbol for other things – for homes, clothes, healthcare, work, hope, justice – all the things that Jesus was always banging on about, the necessities of life, the where-withal to sustain life. Water, too …

We go to great lengths, do we not, to protect our right to control who will get bread. We protect our interests, our shares, our boundaries, our freedom in the markets of the globe at every level …

~ Kathy Galloway

Grace

For this, our daily bread, we thank you God.
Help us to share bread in your world.
Amen

~ Neil Paynter

That none may be hungry

Jesus, Bread of Life
  broken like daal
Be one with the people
  in the brokenness of all our living and loving.
Bless, and be known to us in
  the breaking and sharing of our roti and daal.
Feed us, and feed the world, now and ever more.

Help us so to live, love and share
  that none may be hungry
  and all may eat with each other
  at your Table.

~ Inderjit Bhogal

Willing sharers

Heavenly Father, we thank you for once more providing our daily bread. Have compassion on those who live in poverty and hunger and help us to be more willing sharers and bearers of each other's burdens.

~ Stella Durand

Through the eyes of the hungry

Generous, loving God
Creator of the world we share,
we ask you to give us today our daily bread.

And as we store the crops
and fill the barns
stack the shelves
pile high the tins
and wander the aisles
of supermarket choice

Show us how to see the world
through the eyes of the hungry.
Teach us how to share with all
our daily bread.

~ Linda Jones/CAFOD

Bread of life

Grateful are we for seedtime and harvest,
for joys of eating, for you Lord our guest.
Humbly admitting this table is spread
with more than could be called our daily bread.

Yes, Lord, by bread alone we cannot live,
the bread of life in you, we pray, please give.
Turn the affluent towards sacrifice,
that nourishment for all will suffice.

~ Edward E. Daub

This grace may be sung to the tune of 'Spirit of God descend upon my heart'.

Prayers of concern

Leader: Let us pray.

Let us pray for those who hunger in this land:
whose only kitchen is a soup kitchen,
whose only food is what others don't want,
whose diet depends on luck, not on planning.

(Pause)

Lord, feed your people
using our skills and conscience,
and eradicate from our politics and private lives
the apathy to hunger which comes from over-eating.

Let us pray for the hungry and the fed.

ALL: LORD HAVE MERCY.

Leader: Let us pray for the hungry in other lands,
where economies, burdened by debt,
cannot respond to human need:
or where fields are farmed for our benefit
by low-waged workers courted by starvation.

(Pause)

Lord, feed your people,
even if rulers must cancel debt,
and shareholders lose profit,
or diners restrict their choice
in order that all may be nourished.

Let us pray for the hungry and for the fed.

ALL: LORD HAVE MERCY.

Leader: Let us pray for the hungry for justice,
who document inequalities,
demonstrate against tyranny,
distinguish between need and greed,
and are sometimes misrepresented or persecuted
in the process.

(Pause)

May their labour not be in vain
and may we be counted in their number.

Let us pray for the hungry and the fed.

ALL: LORD HAVE MERCY.

Leader: So, in the presence of the Bread of Life
who refused food for himself
in order to nourish others,
we deepen our devotion by praying his words:

ALL: OUR FATHER IN HEAVEN,
HALLOWED BE YOUR NAME.
YOUR KINGDOM COME,
YOUR WILL BE DONE ON EARTH
AS IN HEAVEN.
GIVE US TODAY OUR DAILY BREAD.
FORGIVE OUR SINS
AS WE FORGIVE THOSE WHO SIN AGAINST US.
SAVE US FROM THE TIME OF TRIAL,
AND DELIVER US FROM EVIL,
FOR THE KINGDOM, THE POWER
AND THE GLORY ARE YOURS,
NOW AND FOR EVER.
AMEN

~ Wild Goose Worship Group

Lord give us bread

Lord give us bread
and let us eat
to give us strength –
and let our strength
help us to work
so that all may share
the bread of Life.

~ Jane Bentley

Bread

A handful of bread
spread out on the wasteland
and a million feathers
beating the air

A little old lady
feeding pigeons –
hunger and loneliness
meeting to share

in a moment of glory
and both were fed
on a cold day in Highgate*
by a handful of bread.

~ Ruth Burgess
*Not the London suburb but an inner-city area of Birmingham.

Be gentle

Be gentle
when you touch bread.
Let it not lie
uncared for … unwanted.
So often
bread is taken for granted.
There is so much beauty
in bread,
beauty of sun and soil
beauty of patient toil.
Winds and rain have caressed it,
Christ so often blessed it.
Be gentle when you touch bread.

(Bread is eaten)

Be loving when you drink wine.
Let its colour, life and beauty be appreciated.
There is so much beauty in wine –
beauty of self-giving, beauty of forgiving.
Winds and rain have caressed it,
Christ so often blessed it.
Be loving when you drink wine.

(Wine is drunk)

~ Graham Sparkes (on behalf of 'Table Fellowship')
  (First section traditional)

Grace

We hold hands as we gather around the table.
We pause. We pray:

Give us this day our daily bread

(Pause)

Be gentle when you touch bread

(Pause)

Loving Creator God, we give thanks that we are able to touch bread.
Let us pause and think of those who have no bread to touch.

Loving Creator God, we give thanks that we are able to eat with joy.
Let us pause and think of those who have no joy to share.

Loving Creator God, we give thanks
as we welcome Jesus Christ, the 'unseen guest', to our table.
Amen

~ Ailsa Maley

(Grace used one lunchtime at the National Assembly of the Uniting Church, Perth, Australia)

Prayer

Loving God, take our hands,
take our lives,
ordinary as wheat or cornmeal,
daily as bread –
our stumbling generosity,
our simple actions,
and find them good enough
to help prepare the feast
for all your people.

~ Christian Aid

Readings:

Exodus 40:22–23
Matthew 6:26
Matthew 14:15–21
Mark 14:22
Luke 11:1–4
Luke 24:30–32
John 6:51

Getting our TEETH into things

Getting one's teeth into things

The mark of Christian spirituality is to get one's teeth into things. 'I was an hungered and ye gave me meat.' ... 'Lord, when saw we Thee an hungered?' ... 'Inasmuch as ye have done it unto the least of these my brethren.'

Painstaking service to humankind's most material needs is the essence of Christian spirituality. Yet it is only the spirit in which we do things that profits anything ...

~ George MacLeod

Grace

God, we thank you for good, nutritious food,
for wine to make us glad,
for friends who love and accept us,
for the freedom to talk and meet together.

We remember the many in the world who are denied these things:

those who are hungry,
those without clean water to drink,
those who are homeless and alone,
those imprisoned for their beliefs.

Loving God, we are so thankful for all that we have.
Help us to get our teeth into things.
Amen

~ Neil Paynter

For all God's people

I was hungry and starving and you were obese;
thirsty, and you were watering your garden;
with no road to follow, and without hope, and you called the police
and were happy when they took me prisoner;
barefoot and with ragged clothing and you were saying
'I will buy something new.'
Sick, and you asked: 'Is it infectious?'
Prisoner, and you said: 'That is where all those of your class should be.'
Lord, have mercy!

~ Latin America/Caribbean, author unknown/CAFOD

Living on nothing

Living on nothing is trying not to see the wretchedness and the despair,
living on nothing is trying not to feel the loss of hope.

Living on nothing is trying not to taste the anger and disappointment.
Living on nothing is trying not to smell the fear.

Living on nothing is trying not to hear the intellectual arguments
    and lofty ideals
about living on nothing
put forward by those who are not living on nothing.

Living on nothing is dying.

~ ATD Fourth World family member

Prayer

We pray for all those living in poverty, struggling to feed their families and to make ends meet; for all who are socially excluded.

We pray for those in power; and for the coming of 'an approach to anti-poverty policies that places on record the capacities and willingness of very poor people to take a major part in initiatives aimed at overcoming poverty'.[1]

We give thanks for this meal and for all the gifts and riches in our lives.

We offer all these prayers in the name of Jesus, who became poor,
and who understands what it's like to be patronised and romanticised.[2]

Jesus Christ, the poor God
of Nazareth, of Pollok, of Muirhouse,[3]
of Stepney, of Tower Hamlets, of King's Cross …
Amen

~ Neil Paynter

The touch of our love
'Making cakes and washing the dishes is love' – James Fraser, L'Arche Inverness

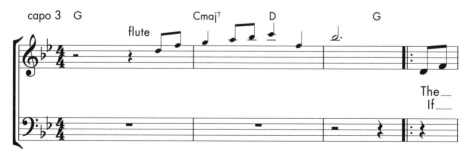

touch of our love A hand in-vi-si-ble;
you do not have Warm feel-ings in your___ heart,

No one can steal joy; That gift in-side from God.
You will ne-ver see The pov-er-ty of God,

God, Pov-er-ty of God.

~ *Text: James Fraser, L'Arche Inverness. Music:* da Noust.

Hunger is torture

Voice: Amnesty International has said, perceptively, that one of the worst forms of torture is hunger.[4]

(Moment of silence)

Prayers of concern (while lighting candles for people and places in the world where there is starvation or hunger).

The Lord's Prayer (each in his or her own language and tradition).

or:

Prayer

O God,
you have made us creatures of this earth,
hungry and thirsty and needy,
that you might satisfy all our longings
with your abundant love.

Satisfy the hunger of our bodies
for food and shelter, health and human touch.
Satisfy the hunger of our spirits
for dignity and freedom
in giving and receiving.
Satisfy the hunger of our minds
to understand our world,
the reasons for its pain,
the ways we are connected to each other.

Satisfy the hunger of our hearts
that all who share this loving earth with us
shall share our satisfaction.
And satisfy the hunger of our hands
to help you make it so

Through Jesus Christ,
Amen.

~ Christian Aid

If the hunger of others

If the hunger of others is not my own,
if the anguish of my neighbour in all its forms
touches me not,
if the nakedness of my brother or sister
does not torment me,
then I have no reason to go to church and live.
Life is this: to love one's neighbour as oneself;
this is the commandment of God.
Love means deeds, not good wishes.
For this reason I commit myself to working
for the necessities of my brothers and sisters.

~ Javier Torres/CAFOD

Bread and butter

It is good enough to talk of God whilst we are sitting here after a nice breakfast and looking forward to a nicer luncheon, but how am I to talk of God to the millions who have to go without two meals a day? To them God can only appear as bread and butter.

~ *Gandhi*

For fairer trade

If it should be, loving Father of all,
that, all unknown to us,
our eating causes others to starve,
our plenty springs from others' poverty
or our choice feeds off others' denial,
then, Lord,
forgive us,
enlighten us,
and strengthen us to work for fairer trade
and just reward. Amen

~ *Donald Hilton*

A grace for our time

O God,
to those who have hunger give bread,
to us who have bread
give hunger for justice.

~ From South America, source unknown
(This grace has been referred to by some as 'A Grace for our time')

Bendice, Señor, nuestro pan

Ben - di - ce, Se - ñor nues - tro pan, y da pan a los que tien - en

ham - bre y ham - bre de jus - ti - cia a los que tien - en

pan. Ben - di - ce Se - ñor nues - tro pan.

~ Music annotation and Spanish transcription: Federico Pagura

The Selkirk grace

Some hae meat and canna eat
and some wad eat that want it
but we hae meat and we can eat
sae let the Lord be thankit.

~ Attributed to Robert Burns[5]

Feed the hungry

... An American diet is a diet of death. The food that God gives us is enough for everyone, everywhere on earth. God did not create a world in which there is hunger. Jesus comes to us again in faith, giving us nothing more than everything we want. In Mark 6, Jesus tells his disciples, even as he tells us, 'You, yourselves, give them something to eat.' With five loaves and a couple fish, Jesus thanks God, the Creator of enough for everyone, and sends his disciples to feed the people. Everyone ate, and there was enough. Twelve baskets of fish and bread were left. There is enough for everyone: it's the miracle of the presence of Christ; it's the goodness of the Creator; it is the movement into liberation that leads us to a life in the wilderness rooted in faith and struggle against oppression. There is enough! There is no reason for hunger in this land. We will never accept hunger, because those who do are blind and have not seen the glorious light that lets us see in darkness. Let us be filled in our hunger! Let us be nourished and strengthened on our journey.

Oppression and greed are the causes of hunger in our land. Power and affluence lead to oppression and greed. Hunger is not a class issue. One thing about rich people is they get hungry. Poor people get hungry. The issue is who gets to eat. This world that God loves so much is filled with people who have too much and others who do not have enough. Some people are consumed by overeating, while others starve.

In Ezekiel 34, God tells the shepherds, the leaders, the policy makers that God is their enemy because they have not cared for the sheep. They have eaten the best grass and trampled what remained. A couple of weeks ago we went out on a Saturday night to check the dumpsters for cardboard because we were spending the night in the backyard. Cardboard is a good insulation against cold ground. We checked the stores in this neighbourhood. Dumpster after dumpster was padlocked. 'You even trample down what you don't eat. You drink the clear water and muddy what you don't drink. My other sheep have to eat the grass you trample down and drink the water that you muddy.'

Our liberating God says, 'When I break my people's chains and set them free from those who have made them slaves, then they will know that I am the Lord their God. I will give them fertile fields and put an end to hunger in the land.'

A primary source of hunger that we face in this land, in this city, in this community, is the disproportion of power that allows some people to have too much money and influence. Their excess comes from the backs and bellies of the poor and the hungry.

A second source of hunger is found in the Book of Isaiah, chapter 55: 'Why do you spend money on what does not satisfy?' What is at the heart of America that drives us to exploit the natural resources of the world? We eat and eat and eat, and are not satisfied. God says, 'Listen to me and do what I say. You will enjoy the best food of all.' Come to me and you will have life. Each of us in our journey must continue to choose life – abundant life – that satisfies as we pour out our lives in servanthood, in solidarity with the oppressed.

Throughout the Bible, God feeds the hungry. Jesus calls us in Matthew 25 to concern ourselves with that work, which is a mark of the gathering of

Christian people. Christians eat and invite all sorts of folk to join them. Fundamentally, the biblical response to the hunger on Butler Street, and in our own lives, is to feed the hungry, to share the food that we have, and to be happy, even when it's only five loaves and two fishes.

Tomorrow morning this community will go to Butler Street, and we will feed the hungry. We will do that in the name of Jesus. We are sent to feed. We have been graced. Though we are still deaf, we have heard little bits. 'Go to Butler Street, feed the hungry. For when you have fed the least of these my sisters and brothers,' says Jesus, 'you've fed me.'

We are taught by Jesus, commanded by God in joyful obedience, day after day, to pray for food. 'Give us this day our daily bread.' The prayer that we must pray for the world is that the plenty will be shared by everyone. We cannot stop praying for our daily bread, believing that there is enough for everyone. It must be shared, distributed, harvested – good, healthy joy for everyone.

God teaches us through the scriptures that we are God's chosen people, who must demand that the hungry be fed. It won't do us any good just to go to Butler Street and serve 250 people every morning, then to come and pray, 'Give us this day our daily bread,' then to go about our usual lives. We must demand that the hungry be fed in the name of God.

You remember the story in Luke when Jesus teaches the disciples how to pray. After he teaches them the words of the Lord's prayer, Jesus suggests prayer is like having a guest late at night. You find that you're out of bread, so you go to your neighbour's house to ask for bread. The neighbour won't come to the door because it's too late. You persist in knocking. Jesus teaches us, in the midst of our going to Butler Street, to join the prophetic community. We become those who won't quit knocking on the doors of City Hall, along the streets of Atlanta, in the state legislature, on the doors of those running this Congress – who won't feed the hungry but who will take their food stamps and their medical care, who suck the life out of the poor.

If we don't feed the sheep at Butler Street, God will be our enemy. But God is not our enemy; God is our Beloved Friend. God empowers us, invites us, and loves us into being those who understand that there's enough for everyone. We understand that hunger is rooted in oppression and in choices about what we do with our lives. We know that this God calls us and sends us to feed the hungry, to pray for food, and to demand that the despicable and hated hunger of so many women and men, boys and girls come to an end.

~ Ed Loring, Open Door Community, Atlanta

Gabi, Gabi

Gabi, Gabi
Bash' abazalwan'
Siyoshiywa khona
Sidal' ubuzalwan'

Praise the Father
Liberator Lord
He frees all the captives
and gives the hungry bread

~ From South Africa

Simple tastes

God, help us serve others rather than our own appetites;
keep us satisfied with simple tastes.
Help us to share our lives with glad and generous hearts.

~ Neil Paynter

May we live more simply

May we live more simply
like the bread.
May we see more clearly
like the water.
May we be more selfless
like the Christ.
Amen

~ A traditional Russian prayer (adapted)

The water of life

O God,
pour out on us the water of life
that we may quench our thirst
and draw our strength from you.
Help us to stand alongside those
who struggle daily for clean water
so that all may be
refreshed and renewed by your love.

~ Christian Aid

Beans and toast

If we are to go for a more equitable sharing of the earth's resources, our own gauge of sufficiency must show a dramatic drop. 'We must live simply that others may simply live,' said the Dean in his sermon – and went back to his roast beef and two veg. Good news to the poor which implies beans and toast instead of roast beef will not be welcome. But that is the way of the Kingdom. This was instinctively seen in the early church (see Acts 2:44 ff., 4:3–7).

Evangelism must be quite central for us. What the world needs to see, illustrated in lifestyles as well as in words, is good news. It needs to recognise that Kingdom priorities mean life for the world and other ways are ways of death.

It needs to seek first the Kingdom. Only when the love of Christ constrains them will people be able to surrender that unfair share of the world's resources which has left others in squalor and voicelessness and suffering.

A sign that we are at least on the way will be the joy and thanksgiving with which we live daily, eat our food, wear what clothes we need, appreciate shelter, family and friends, and are a sign of that freedom from anxiety which Jesus commended when he spoke of the lilies of the field and birds of the air.

~ *Ian M. Fraser*

The simplicity of food

The simplicity of food reminds us that we have chosen a way that involves sharing with those most in need. Matthew 25:34–40

~ *Brother Roger, Taizé*

Nourish our anger

Food three times a day. Some food every third day.
We live in an unjust world.
As our bodies are nourished, nourish our anger at injustice, we pray.
Amen

~ Ian M. Fraser

In this world of plenty

God, we remember those who are hungry
in this world of plenty.

We remember those who are lonely,
starving for closeness and love
in crowded cities.

And we think of those living without the sustaining energy
and goodness of your word.

God, we thank you for the gift of this food,
for the gift of friends,
and for the gift of your son,

who came to bring justice, healing
and peace.

Bless this meal.

May it give us strength
to do your work in the world.
Amen

~ Neil Paynter

Light a candle

Light a candle in a dark room
to reveal the goodness and plenty of this table.
The meal prepared for us to eat.
The wine served for us to drink.

Light a candle in a dark world
to remember those who are hungry and thirsty.
Those who hunger for food and justice.
Those who thirst for water and for love.

Light a candle to welcome the kingdom
where there is enough for everyone
and everyone is present.
And the blessing of God gives us life.

~ Graham Sparkes (on behalf of 'Table Fellowship')

A greater sharing

As we taste this food,
may we remember those who go hungry;
as we are nourished,
may we find energy to work
for a greater sharing in the world.

~ Jan Sutch Pickard

To work for justice

We have food.
Others are hungry.
May we use the strength
this food gives
to work for justice.

~ Ruth Burgess

Feed the world

We depend on the world to feed us, Lord God.
Let our concern be, in turn, to feed the world. Amen

~ Ian M. Fraser

To do your work

Lord Jesus,
thank you for this food before us.
May it give us strength
to do your work.
Amen

~ Mark Westbrook

Swords into ploughshares

Bountiful, giving God,
we thank you for the food that we are about to share here.
We remember with sorrow that your gifts are not shared fairly
across the world,
that every minute a million pounds is spent on weapons of war,
while 25 children die because of hunger.[6]
Strengthen our bodies with this food.
And strengthen our resolve to work for a world of justice and of peace
where swords are hammered into ploughshares,
bread replaces bombs,
and all your children can eat and be satisfied.
Amen

~ *Helen Boothroyd*

Plates and hearts

May we whose plates and hearts
are full
be always thankful
and work tirelessly to make a better world
for those whose plates and hearts
are empty.

~ *Joy Mead*

Help us to bring change

~ Music & text: Pat Livingstone, Oran

This piece has a two-bar ostinato whilst the melody is sung above reminding us of the urgency of the need for change so that food is fairly distributed throughout the northern and southern hemispheres.

When I give food to the poor

When I give food to the poor
they call me a saint.
When I ask why the poor have no food,
they call me a communist.

~ *Dom Helder Camara/CAFOD*

Short

Take, eat, digest, do justice. Amen

~ *David Coleman*

A prayer of gratitude

Grant, eternal God, that we who are amongst those who most readily speak your name be as quick to sacrifice and share so that a prayer of gratitude may encircle the world. Amen

~ *Donald Hilton*

When none shall hunger

Loving God, while we eat, others starve. To labour the guilt we feel would spoil this meal so generously set before us by your love and the work of friends. Instead, we pledge our continued giving and service to hasten the day when none shall hunger and all shall be satisfied. Amen

~ *Donald Hilton*

Grace

Isten, God of our confessing.
Isten, Light in deep distressing.
Isten, Grant to us thy blessing.
One, the blessed God we cherish,
may this food our bodies nourish
faith and freedom ever flourish.
Amen

~ Adapted by Rev. Richard Boeke from a free translation by Rev. Josef Kaszoni
of an ancient Hungarian hymn. 'Egy az Isten' means God is One.

As we wait for the day

As we wait for the day when the poor are no longer hungry,
as we wait for the day when farmers are treated fairly,
as we wait for the day when the fortunate are no longer greedy,
as we wait for the day when the earth is treated with respect;
Lord God, we are so grateful for what you have provided.
Amen

~ Peter Graystone/Christian Aid

Readings:

Psalm 14:4
Isaiah 55:2
Ezekiel 3:1–3
Amos 5:6–15, 18–24
Matthew 5:6
Matthew 25:31–46
Luke 16:19–31

Graces for
EATING ALONE

I eat alone

I eat alone, God.
So please join me
at my table
and be my guest.

~ Ruth Burgess

A grace for eating alone

Blessed be the silence of this meal
Blessed be the solitude of this eating
Blessed be the company of unseen presences
Blessed be my single table

~ Nicola Slee

We do not eat this meal alone

We do not eat this meal alone
but with those who share the table.

We do not eat this meal alone
but with people who prepared it.

We do not eat this meal alone
but with all who grew or traded it,
inspected or transported it.

We do not eat this meal alone
but with those who do not have enough
and those who have too much.

We do not eat this meal alone
but with our generous Provider,
the Parent of the human race
and Maker of our planet.

Amen

~ Brian Woodcock

Readings:

Psalm 16:7–8
Psalm 34:18
Psalm 145:18
Isaiah 43:1–3
Matthew 28:19–20
John 10: 27–28
Acts 17:27–28

Christ our HOST
Christ our GUEST

Persevere

We persevere, a pilgrim band;
we're called –
to live in hope, not fear,
to welcome all we scorn or hate
within our heart, among our kin;
a covenant of love proclaim.

~ da *Noust*

Music: Mayenziwe7, South African melody

Come as you are

Don't be something to impress me
for I love you as you are.
I have made you as I want you,
why be something that you're not?

Come as you are.
All I ask is that you bring to me your heart.
I have made you to love me,
and all I ask is love.
Your ideas of perfection leave me dry.

Bring me your heart
(Bring me your heart)
and live in mine.

~ *Words and music: Angela Dodds/da Noust*

Grant us the grace

Lord grant us the grace to be happy.
The grace to find peace of mind
To walk in the ways of Jesus,
leaving selfishness behind;
To open our house to strangers,
our table to those in need.
And give us the grace and the strength, Lord,
to follow wherever you lead.
Amen

~ *Sheila E. Auld*

Good excuse (Abram and Sarah's grace)

For guests
Who give us the excuse

For food that builds friends
From strangers

For news
That brings laughter

For life
That makes life new

For tongue-tip expectation
May we live thanks. AMEN

~ *David Coleman*

They had virtually nothing, yet ...

We had joy and satisfaction too – Fatmeh, a little girl who at six months weighed only four kilogrammes, became an eight-month beauty with bows in her hair. She went home weighing only 1.8kg to her family's tent of old sacks fifteen kilometres from the nearest village. Her Beduin family has never been allowed to build a house on their own land as there is an Israeli army camp nearby. Over the years they have become poorer and poorer. They no longer have the traditional Beduin tent of goat's hair, which is cool in the summer and warm and dry in the winter. Fortunately Fatmeh's mother was able to breast-feed her and she thrived. The family had almost nothing – a donkey to carry the water they must walk miles to fetch, and a few hens – yet they insisted on brewing up tea and pressed me to take some of their precious dried yoghourt. They had virtually nothing, yet they gave us traditional Beduin hospitality ...

~ Dr Runa Mackay

Angels in disguise

1 Kings 17:8–16

As the poor widow welcomed Elijah,
let us be open to the richness and miracle in meeting.

As Abraham and Sarah welcomed passing strangers,
let us entertain the possibility of angels in disguise,

and of encounters that leave us laughing:
strangely blessed with new life.

God bless this meal and company.

~ Neil Paynter

Trim the cruisie's failing light (Rune of Barra)

Trim the cruisie's failing light;
the Son of God shall pass tonight,
shall pass at midnight dreary,
the Son of Mary weary.

Lift the sneck and wooden bar
and leave the stranger's door ajar
lest he may tarry lowly,
the Son of Mary holy.

Sweep the hearth and pile the peat
and set the board with bread and meat;
the son of God may take it,
the Son of Mary break it.

~ Translated by Murdoch MacLean

Perpetual welcome

Eternal God,
may the hospitality we now enjoy
in this home and at this table
be a sign to us
of your perpetual welcome to this earth.
And may the gratitude we feel for all that is set before us
be as a prayer of thanksgiving to you;
the giver of all that is good. Amen

~ *Donald Hilton*

St Columba and hospitality

The reputation of the community on Iona grew quickly, and curious visitors and pilgrims flocked to the island. Hospitality was a sacred monastic obligation, and Adomnán reports how Columba cancelled a fast day to give hospitality to 'a certain troublesome guest'. He also recounts the saint's legendary ability to sense when a guest was about to arrive. For example,

> On a day when the tempest was fierce and the sea exceedingly boisterous, the saint gave orders, saying, 'Prepare the guest chamber quickly and draw water to wash the stranger's feet.' One of the brethren enquired, 'Who can cross the Sound safely on so perilous and stormy a day!' The saint made answer: 'The Almighty has given a calm evening in this tempest to a certain holy and excellent man who will arrive here among us before evening.' And lo! That same day the ship for which the brethren had some time been looking out arrived accord-

ing to the saint's prediction and brought St Cainnech. The saint went down with his brethren to the landing place and received him with all honour and hospitality.

Hospitality was sacred, because Christ was in the stranger. The Gaelic Rune of Hospitality puts it thus:

We saw a stranger yesterday,
we put food in the eating place,
drink in the drinking place,
music in the listening place
and, with the sacred name of the triune God,
he blessed us and our house, our cattle and our dear ones.
As the lark says in her song:
Often, often, often, goes Christ in the stranger's guise.

~ *Ron Ferguson*

Help us to hear you

Listen! I stand at the door and knock;
if any hear my voice and open the door,
I will come into their house and eat with them.
And they will eat with me.
(Rev 3:20)

Jesus, help us to hear you:

in the appeals and protests
of refugees and asylum seekers,

facing closed borders and
locked in detention;

in the cries and shouts
of homeless people

left out in the cold.

Open our hearts to all who are exiled and outcast.
Lord, come in!

~ Neil Paynter

A neighbourhood

I remember my neighbourhood in Ottawa, Canada – the diversity of it. I used to love going into all the Chinese grocery stores: there were ducks in the windows, strange vegetables and fruit, mysterious dried things in packets. I bought tea once and it had cicadas in it. There was a Caribbean food and music shop. I made friends with the man who worked there and he turned me on to reggae. Hot, Scotch bonnet peppers. 'Careful now, mon.' They sold records and tapes, all imported – Burning Spear, rare Bob Marley. He explained to me all about Rastafarianism and I-tal food. How I-tal food contained no chemicals or preservatives, nothing 'contaminated by the hands of Babylon'. For lunch you could just go grab a couple home-made vegetable samosas from the Indian food shop and you were happy. The owner's wife made them and they were delicious hot or cold, walking along, taking everything in. We asked for her recipe and her daughter wrote it out for us. The inside of the shop was heady with the smell of spilled spices: cumin, coriander, cloves, turmeric, fennel, fenugreek ... I used to go in sometimes just to say hello and smell! The Middle Eastern bakery made their own pita bread and zatar. You could stand at the window and watch it coming out of the old belt oven. Then go in and buy it warm and fresh, with some hummus, and olives they fished out of plastic pails. You could get fat green olives, or tarry black olives. Rolled in red pepper. Greek feta or Bulgarian feta – the Bulgarian was creamier. Both were good, and salty. The grandmother served us speaking loud and fast, laughing and waving her hands full of silver rings. There was an Iranian shop next door where you could buy a sweet, flat bread and a dessert like baklava. The baklava was so good honey dripped out when you bit into it. All along the streets you could easily buy vegetables like cassava, okra, bokchoy … I hardly ever went to the Babylonian grocery store, with its neat, tidy streets lined with cans and boxes, muzak, nothing to explore, discover or challenge you. We tried to support a corner shop, which a Korean family owned. Our downstairs neighbours were from Vietnam and their daughter, Kim, would come up in the evenings and we'd help her with her homework. We had Italian neighbours across the street who made their own wine. We were known as 'the hippies'. The neighbourhood was full of refugees and asylum seekers. There were posters up everywhere. For demos against the massacre in Tiananmen Square, against the Gulf War: 'No Blood For Oil!', for an El Salvadorean solidarity night in the Community Centre. You always felt welcome. And privileged. One of my friends had been sick and was going to an acupuncturist. He swore by ginseng. There was a Zen Buddhist meditation centre, a Greek Orthodox church, a mosque with a minaret that looked so beautiful with the sun setting behind it. For a moment you forgot what country you were in. There were restaurants everywhere. We had our favourites: Vietnamese, Thai, Cantonese, Szechwan. We got to know the regional tastes and flavours. Menus were in all different languages. There was a tapas bar, where you could go drink and dance late and a man named Enrico played passionate and frenzied flamenco guitar. There was a quiet Ethiopian restaurant where we went to talk about love and life. It was great to tear into injera bread and to eat with our hands. There were trattorias, and cafes where you could go sip cappucino and spend the whole lazy, slow Sunday afternoon sitting talking to friends, while the men in the back room smoked and played cards and watched soccer on satellite TV; there were squid in jars, bottles of olive oil the sun shone through; in summertime they sold gelato and pizza out on the patio. No one in the neighbourhood dressed the same. There were berkas, saris, sandals. Proud African women wrapped in the most beautiful, richly-patterned fabrics strolled the poor streets with aristo-cratic dignity. The neighbourhood was an oasis in a city full of American fast-food restaurants, shopping malls with all the same shops selling all the same things, suburbs that spread and ate the healthy green space.

Sadly, though, it wasn't always a place of life. One long, hot summer there was a shooting; one dark, icy winter a suicide: someone killed in a family argument; someone sick and tired of waiting, waiting for their fate to be decided.

Living in that neighbourhood made us want to travel and to taste life, made us want to help the asylum seekers and refugees whose moving and inspiring stories we'd had the privilege of hearing. Living in that neigh-bourhood made us want to work for one world. One world of amazing diversity and respect.

~ Neil Paynter

Prayer

Dear God, we thank you for
the richness, gifts and contributions
of different cultures

We thank you for:

Nelson Mandela
Archbishop Desmond Tutu
Aung San Suu Kyi
Mahatma Gandhi

For Ray Charles singing *Georgia* and
Little Richard singing *Tutti Frutti Oh Rudy*

For the vocal harmonies of Ladysmith Black Mambazo

For Boogie woogie
be bop
jazz
rap
funk
soul
rock 'n' roll

Salsa clubs
the samba
spirituals and voices
deep and profound as wells of living water

For the heady smell of the Indian grocers
for cardamom, saffron, cloves
jasmine, patchouli, sandalwood

For the music of accents
dance of gestures
communication of smiles

For the lined landscapes of beautiful faces

For kebabs
hummus
baklava
goulash
won ton soup
warm naan bread
tandoori
sweet and sour
rice and peas and curried goat

For Greek delicatessens
Arabic delicatessens
Italian delicatessens
For delicatessens!

For gold jewellery against black skin
the sound of reggae from the car repair shop
the pungent, sour smell of indigo-dyed cloth
the blast and blare of Notting Hill Carnival

~ Neil Paynter and others

Jesus's best friends

… We have turned the neighbourhoods into war zones. We purchase ever bigger breeds of dogs and security systems that blurt bell-like screams when shadows dance in our yards. We construct higher fences topped with barbed wire and we beg the mayor to raise property taxes to pay meaner police to enforce meaner laws. What have we done? We have built more prisons and doubled the prison population in the United States in one short decade. We join associations to stop the bum-bombs from entering our neighbourhoods; we turn against those who feed, shelter, and help the dying Christ. 'Get them out of my sight! Off the porch! From my sidewalk!' How little different is the cry today from the hostile chant of the crowd choosing between Jesus and the thief: 'Crucify him! Crucify him!'

And so they said:

'Hey, Mr Bus Driver,
There's a bomb on the bus!'
'Yes, Mr Bus Driver.'

And this bus is the US of A.
This bus is the Church of Jesus Christ
The Synagogue of Yahweh
The Mosque of Allah

This bus is Atlanta, Georgia,
Peachtree, Ponce de Leon, and Pryor Streets.

If we don't defuse
The bus with justice

If we don't turn the bus around
put the wheels on the King's Highway

If we don't stop telling lies
and calling Jesus's best friends:

    bums
    whores
    lazy bastards

punks
niggers
animals
crazies
winos
rats

If we don't repent
Change this city into Beloved Community

If we don't find Jesus Christ
in the back of the bus
in the soup-kitchen lines

Then ...

The bomb is going to blow up
And we
in our pitiful rags and riches

our college degrees and fabulous
careers
our houses, cars, and bank accounts

Will be dead.

Or

We can rid the land of lovelessness and fear
Where no one is a bum or bomb
Where everyone has enough
Where justice is our security
and we love one another.

'Ain't no bums
ain't no bombs
on this bus,' says Jesus.

'Follow me.'

~ Ed Loring

Grace

Lord Jesus, you stand at the door and knock.
May we hear you knocking and invite you in to feast with us. Amen

~ John Newton, Worth Abbey Lay Community

Be our guest

Food prepared with love,
places set with care.
Come Lord Jesus, be our guest.

But don't let us imagine
that you travel alone.[8]

Lord, help us to make room for your friends:
for those who thirst,
those who hunger.
Amen

~ Neil Paynter

God bless this space

As Martha worked with concern and attention
and Mary stopped and sat in stillness to listen

let us make around ourselves
space comfortable and warm as a hearth fire glowing;

within our hearts
room to receive a guest.

God bless this space and time together.

~ Neil Paynter

In the kitchen

Jesus, you visited homes
of ordinary folk like us.
You sat in kitchens
and talked about life and death
and who would do the washing up.
You invited yourself to tea,
you asked for a drink of water,
you made a faith meal go further.

For the cup of water given in your name
for the cup of tea
poured out in fellowship,

for our ministry of hospitality here –
we thank you, Lord of love.
Amen

~ Jan Sutch Pickard

Moment of infinite grace

Jesus, when you were a guest at meals
amazing things happened:

water turned to wine
five thousand were fed
a lost soul came home.

Jesus, help us to remember
that wherever two or three are gathered you are present,
and so are among us now:

here in this place
and moment of

infinite grace
and
possibility.

Amen

~ Neil Paynter

Jesus, be present

Jesus, be present at our meal
just as you once went home
to eat with Zacchaeus –
and may salvation be served with the soup!

~ Jan Sutch Pickard

To share what we have

Lord, Zacchaeus welcomed you to his home
and you were happy to be there,
though many scorned you for eating with sinners.
With Zacchaeus, give us the wish
to share what we have with others
and bless our table with your healing presence.
Amen

~ Pax Christi

Christ our Host

Luke 24:13–34

George MacLeod invariably said the following grace:

'Christ our Host
Christ our Guest. Amen'

~ From Murdoch Mackenzie

Lord of Joy, come be our guest

1. Gläd-jens Her-re, var en gäst vid vårt bord i dag.

Gör vår mål-tid till en fest ef-ter ditt be-hag.

Glädjens Herre, var en gäst
vid vårt bord I dag.
Gär vår måltid till en fest
efter ditt behag.

För de gåvor som du ger
tackar vi dig nu.
Gud, som hör förrän vi ber,
prisad vare du!

Lord of Joy, come be our guest,
as we share this bread.
In your presence, food is blessed,
soul and body fed.

All the gifts that show your care
we receive with grace.
To you, Lord, who hear each prayer
we give thanks and praise.
Amen

~ Text & music: H D Stern. Translation from the Swedish: Victoria Rudebark

Stay with us Lord

Stay with us Lord,
since the day is far spent and night is coming;
kindle our hearts on the way,
that we may recognise you in the scriptures,
in the breaking of the bread,
and in each other.
Amen

~ Iona Abbey Worship Book

Grace

How did I come to be seated at this table?
How did I come to be eating of this bread?
I am not worthy that you should serve me
yet I will sit and eat.

~ Nicola Slee

Welcome each other

Welcome each other as he welcomed you.
Sharing your life to the glory of God.
Live in the spirit of covenant love.
Welcome each other as Christ welcomed you.

~ Tune: Slane, Irish 8th century. Words: da Noust (based on Romans 15:7)

Sun behind all suns

Almighty God, Sustainer:
sun behind all suns,
soul behind all souls,
everlasting reconciler of our whole beings:
Show to us in everything we touch and in everyone we meet
the continued assurance of Thy presence round us:
lest ever we should think Thee absent.
In created things Thou art there.
In every friend we have
the sunshine of Thy presence is shown forth.

~ George MacLeod

May we be good stewards

We thank you, generous Lord
for the gifts which supply our table.
Keep us mindful of your hospitality
which sustains the whole creation.
May we be good stewards,
guarding the rights of others as our own.
Through Jesus Christ our Lord,
giver of all life and saviour of the world.
Amen

~ Rt Rev Michael Hare Duke

Readings:

Genesis 18:1–15
Leviticus 19:33–34
1 Kings 17:8–24
Matthew 2:13–15
Luke 10: 38–42
Luke 19:1–10
Hebrews 13:1–2

Family,
Friends,
FELLOWSHIP

This waiting moment

Thank you, God, for the moment
before the meal begins.

For the emptiness within us,
the table before us,
the people around us,
and the smell of fresh food in the air.

For this moment,
this waiting moment,
this moment of promise and gratitude,
before the meal begins.

Amen

~ *Brian Woodcock*

A family grace

Our mealtime ritual is the following:

A reading (this can be anything and is chosen for appropriateness).

A pause.

Lighting a candle (placed in sand from Iona's north beach) for the person
sitting on your left.

Grace:
In this meal may we grow in fellowship with each other

and use the energy it gives us
to build a world of beauty, justice, peace
and fun.

~ *George Casley*

Lord of Life

Lord of Life
we celebrate your countless gifts,
in days and nights,
in rainbows and rain,
in touch, dream and smile,
in partners who love,
in kids who cuddle,
in grannies who listen,
in friends who care,
in dogs that lick,
in hands that sew,
in food on the table;
yet above all,
in your coming among us,
walking our roads,
calling our names,
enfolding our lives,
inviting us home.

~ *Peter Millar*

Strong, sheltering God

Strong, sheltering God,
we bless you for all the beautiful things of home;
warmth and shelter when the wind outside is bitter
food for the body and for the soul
treasured gifts and treasured memories
stability, acceptance, care.
We bless you for the chance to be ourselves
for the tasks that weave the pattern of our days
for the sweet, familiar round of ordinary things.
Blessed are you strong, sheltering God.

~ Kathy Galloway

A family prayer

There is great significance in that little word 'our' ... nowhere in our Lord's prayer does the word 'my' come in. It is a family prayer addressed to 'our father', in which we recognise ourselves as brothers and sisters. To get away from our persistent selfishness we must cultivate the sense of the great family to which we are being admitted by God's call to us to be His children. So when we pray for bread to satisfy our own needs, we are to remember the needs of the great family to which we belong. Once the sense of family is awakened we recognise what a monstrous thing it is that one third of the family should have more to eat than is good for them, while two thirds are in danger daily of starvation. The iniquity is aggravated by the great storehouses in which we lock away our wheat and butter mountains, while so many of our brothers and sisters with their little children wither away for lack of food ... The wrong is aggravated by the fact that we are pouring so much of our technological resources and treasure into making weapons devised for killing, that we have little left over for serving the desperate needs of our fellows and making the world a better place. We are spending 22 times as much on arms that may well destroy the world as we are spending on the means of constructive development. Whenever we pray 'Give us this day our daily bread', we should remember our Heavenly Father who hears the cry of the hungry.

~ The Very Rev. Dr George Reid

The Lord's Prayer
(each in his or her own language and tradition)

Lord, if this day

Lord,
if this day you have to correct us,
put us right, not out of anger
but with a mother and father's love.
So may we, your children,
be kept free of falseness and foolishness.

~ From Mexico

Continue to remind us

For friends,
for family,
for food,
for a future in your name,
we give you thanks, Lord,
but we ask you to continue to remind us
of those who have none of these things.
Amen

~ Ewan Aitken

G-R-A-C-E

Good food
Ready to be eaten,
And friends around the table.
Christ Jesus
Encircle us and bless us.

~ Ruth Burgess

The sound of bread breaking

Thank you God:

for the music of a table being set
for the laughter of young children
for the voices of old friends

for the sound of bread
breaking.

God bless this meal and time together.

~ Neil Paynter

For food, for friends

Thank you God
for food
for friends
for time to relax and share.

~ Ruth Burgess

For time to share

God, thank you for time to stop
and sit down.

Time to share with best friends,
savour conversation,
appreciate good food.

May this meal and company
strengthen and refresh us on our journeys.
Amen

~ Neil Paynter

Praise be to God

Praise be to God for this meal before us;
praise be to God for water and wine;
praise be to God for friends to eat with;
praise be to God for blessing this time.

~ Chris Polhill

We name your name

Eternal God,
we name your name,
we live your love,
we greet your gifts,
we feel your forgiveness,
we know your life
and we give you thanks.
Amen

~ Ewan Aitken

True refreshment

May our conversation be as good as the food we eat,
our friendship be as rich,
and our stories as varied as our taste.
May this time together be true refreshment,
a draught from the well-spring of kindness,
and a feast to satisfy our human need.
Amen

~ Donald Hilton

In You we are transformed

Pain, distress, weariness and grief
may be present round this table,
but in You we are transformed
through all that you provide
and for this we thank You
Great God in our midst.
Amen

~ *Yvonne Morland*

Body and soul

Bless our bodies as we eat this food,
bless our souls as we dine together.
Fill our glasses with wine,
fill our hearts with friendship.

~ *Chris Polhill*

An African saying

Eat and drink together
talk and laugh together
enjoy life together
but never call it friendship
until you have wept together

Stay with us, healer of fear

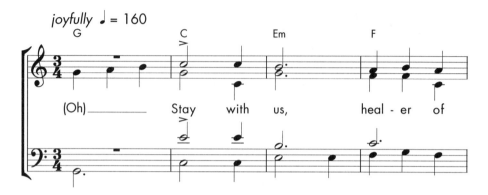

joyfully ♩ = 160

(Oh)____ Stay with us, heal - er of

fear, Come to our ta - ble, share our meal;

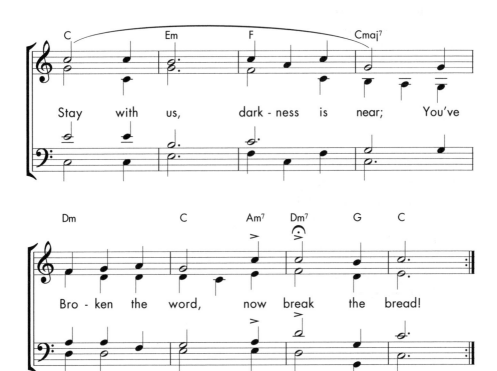

Stay with us, dark - ness is near; You've

Bro - ken the word, now break the bread!

~ *Music & text:* **da** *Noust*

Grace

For wining and dining
friendship and laughter
we praise God's holy name.

~ Chris Polhill

Spread your cloak

For your gifts good God
on this table, in our lives.
For your presence good God
in our hearts and in our homes.
We give thanks, yet we remember
    the lonely ones tonight.
Spread your cloak around them,
    keep them safe from harm.
Amen

~ Yvonne Morland

Grace

For food that gives us life
and friends that give us love
of life,
thanks be to God.

~ Joy Mead

That we may be renewed

Loving God,
bless our food and drink,
our friendship and our laughter,
that we may be renewed
in body, mind and spirit
to work together
for the coming of your kingdom
of justice, love and peace. Amen

~ Maureen Edwards

Food and friendship

From food and the ability to enjoy it
and from friendship and the ability to feed from it,
we are nurtured, Lord.
Amen

~ Ewan Aitken

Favourite meals

Voice 1: My favourite meal was at college with my housemates. It was the end of the year and everyone had run out of money. So, we decided to throw all the food we had left together, and make this big pot of soup – there was some wine and bread left. We just kept throwing things in the pot – whatever we could find in the fridge, in the back of the cupboard. When we looked down into it finally we couldn't stop laughing. It looked revolting! It was a brilliant night though. We just talked and ate soup. Talked about all the funny things that had happened, the serious things.

Talked about all we'd shared during the year. When I speak to those people now, on the phone or by e-mail, we all still remember that night. The night that the soup and the laughter never seemed to run out.

Voice 2: I remember working in Africa. Being invited to a meal, the incredible hospitality and welcome. A big pot in the middle and everyone sharing. Eating with your hands – the deftness of it. Beans with sauce and bread. On occasions, goat. Drum music and dancing.

Voice 3: My favourite meal was New Year's Day with family. We had fish fingers, and beans and chips. It was just so relaxed and chilled.

Voice 4: In Peru we were invited to stay with a family, and it was just so nice and such a privilege. It was on an island in Lake Titicaca. Four, or five, thousand metres high up maybe. They could only grow potatoes up there. Potatoes and a special kind of rice. The mother cooked a meal for us: just potatoes and rice. So simple. Potatoes from the garden. Nothing fancy. So simple and close to the earth, but it was one of the best meals I've ever eaten. It was just the feeling of being there – the place where potatoes came from originally; sitting in the kitchen; the men knitting these beautiful, colourful hats and the women carrying sacks of potatoes, walking in sandals made from car tyres. How they had so many different ways of cooking potatoes. The way their faces were beautiful and furrowed like the earth. Their hands, dark and rough. Like the earth.

Grace

For food and friends and moments when we can sense
    your kingdom breaking through
Thank you, amazing God.
Amen

Eat and enjoy, and share memories of some favourite meals.

~ Neil Paynter

(Neil Paynter, Alan Hawkins, Helen O'Donnell, Camilla Björkborn)

Together

For this eating together
this drinking together
we thank you together
Amen

~ Sheila E. Auld

God of work and rest

The fellowship of the table has a festive quality. It is a constantly recurring reminder in the midst of our everyday work of God resting after his work ... Our life is not only travail and labour, it is also refreshment and joy in the goodness of God. We labour, but God nourishes and sustains us. And this is the reason for celebrating ... Through our daily meals he is calling us to rejoice, to keep holiday in the midst of our working day.

~ Dietrich Bonhoeffer

Grace

For food and fellowship to nourish and refresh us,
God of work and of rest
we celebrate you.
Amen

~ Neil Paynter

Giving God

For fresh air and fellowship, for fun and friendship, for faith and for this food, we thank You, giving God. Amen

~ Helen Boothroyd

God at the centre

God at the centre
God at the edge
God round about us
God in between us
God ever present.

Thank you for our food.
Thank you for our fellowship.

Be with your little ones tonight.

Amen

~ Yvonne Morland

Thank you, Lord

Thank you, Lord, for this meal,
for the rich gifts of this table,
for food and drink to give us strength.
But we cannot live by bread alone.
We share it together
because we need each other

gathered around this table.
All: We need …
Response: And I need you.
  (The group name each person in turn
  who then makes the response.)
Thank you, Lord, for one another and for this meal.

~ *Graham Sparkes (on behalf of 'Table Fellowship')*

The gift of one another

As we gather round this table
may we be open to receive
the gift of one another
through whom you call us to believe
in your community of Love,
O God of our lives.
Amen

~ *Yvonne Morland*

We rejoice

Creator God
We rejoice in the beauty of your world around us.
We rejoice at the smell and taste of food to warm, sustain and satisfy us.
We rejoice in the fellowship we find with each other,
and we praise you.
Amen

~ *Helen Boothroyd*

Ordinary IV

God of all goodness,
through the breaking of bread together
you strengthen the bonds that unite us in love.
Bless us, and these your gifts.
Grant that as we sit down together at table in joy and sincerity,
we may grow always closer in the bonds of love.

We ask this through Christ our Lord. Amen

~ From Dom Aidan Murray, OSB, The Worth Abbey Lay Community

The aesthetic of hunger is a lie

Ah, the thrill of anticipation an odour can bring!

So eat hearty, mates. Rend that chicken limb from limb.
Bread is made to chase gravy round a plate. If the art
of manners should be a passing thought, let it pass.
Starvation improves no one; the aesthetic of hunger is a lie.

A moment of recognition, if you like, or pause
but no more. Gratification can be delayed too long.
Protect your pleasure from unfocused guilt.
Enjoy yourself. Celebrate. Love one another.

~ Robert Davidson

All who are hungry

Lord,
we thank you for this time together.
We thank you for this food and for the love and the care
   with which it has been prepared.
We ask that, in your mercy, you will feed all who are hungry at this time.
Amen

~ Sandy Yule/John Bartholomew

Prayer

Jesus, help us to serve one another,
to love as you loved.

~ Neil Paynter

For wholesome, earthy food

For wholesome, earthy food
and the flow
of heady conversation

Thank you, Jesus.

~ Neil Paynter

A simple meal

When Christians gather at the table today they continue a tradition that began with Jesus and the first Christians. It is a tradition of resistance to and subversion of the powers of the world. It unmasks the hollow logic and vain constructions of fallen humanity, contesting and disrupting all the spaces where alienation and domination still prevail. The table tradition makes the hope of God's reign a reality amidst the voices of despair, and brings healing and reconciliation to those who know only violence and hate. It opens every closed door.

Remarkably, all of this happens in the most common event – a simple meal. Amidst the principalities and powers, a meal may seem small and ineffective. But, as we have discovered on the streets, such small, embodied signs of God's reign show us the way and give us hope for the journey ...

~ Stanley P. Saunders

Grace

Jesus, long ago, your followers met to share bread
and to gather their strength against the powers.

May this food and companionship give us encouragement and strength
to resist and engage the powers of today.
Amen

~ Neil Paynter

Prayer

Set our hearts on fire with love to thee
O Christ, that in that flame we may love thee
and our neighbour as ourselves.

~ Eastern Orthodox prayer

Readings:

Ruth 1:16–17
1 Samuel 18:1–3
1 Kings 8:1
Luke 8:19–21
John 1:12–13
Colossians 3:12–14
Hebrews 13:16

God's
CREATION

Opening prayer

Creator,
we give thanks that you long to
sustain us, just as in the time
of our ancestors you cared for us.
Shield and care for us
as an eagle cares for its young.

We give thanks that you come to
bring healing and nourishment to all.

Help us to be open to all the ways
you nourish us.

May we be at peace with each other.

~ Joyce Carlson

The wonder and mystery

For the wonder and mystery of God's creation,
for our oneness with the air we breathe
and all that sustains us,
we give thanks. Amen

~ Maureen Edwards

Creator Spirit

Creator Spirit, we thank you
for food to nourish us,
to strengthen and sustain us,
to fit us for your service. Amen

~ *Jean Williams*

A prayer of thanks for Creation

Creator of the universe, we praise you for all creation.
We thank you
for the earth, giver and sustainer of life
for the sun who gives us light and life and warmth
for the moon and stars who light our way in the night
for the winged animals
for the animals that swim in the lakes, rivers, and oceans
and for those who walk on land.

We also thank you
for the plants that grow in the ground
    and the food and protection they provide;
for the people who walk beside us and live with us in our homes.

This is the family you have given us and we praise your wonderful creation.

~ *Ellen Cook*

Twentieth-century grace

Thank you for the food we ate,
for monosodium glutamate
and every other additive
our grateful thanks to You we give.
For stacks of cans of fruit and veg
and every plastic coated wedge
of cheese and sliced bread wrapped in wax
and instant meals contained in packs.
For all the items in deep freeze
we give you thanks on bended knees.
For pallid calves and battery hens
we raise to You our glad amens.

We must confess, we'd really rather
give thanks unto our Heavenly Father
for crusty loaves of wheaten bread
and golden butter thickly spread,
for honey dripping from the comb
and eggs from fowls allowed to roam,
for foamy milk, fresh from the cow
– but things are very different now.
From what we'll eat another day
protect us from all harm, we pray.

~ Kathleen White/Christian Ecology Link

Christian Ecology link is a multi-denominational UK Christian movement for people concerned about the environment. Founded in 1981, it has worship materials, leaflets, workshops, conferences, local groups, campaigns and a thrice yearly magazine called 'Green Christians'. Its website – www.christian-ecology.org.uk – has many resources and provides news of environmental and Christian events.

We cannot eat money

Only when the last tree has died
and the last river has been poisoned
and the last fish has been caught
will we realise that we cannot eat money.

~ From the Native American tradition, 19th-century Cree Indian

Our ancestors

Our ancestors taught us to share what we gather in a day.
We must keep the forest as the home of animals
but also for pure water and air.
The only reason it still exists
is that we have taken care that it is not destroyed.
We need the trees for thatch,
for medicines and because they provide fruit.

~ Shibo indigenous people, Peru/CAFOD

The seventh generation

How unlike the North American woodland Indians we are. They often think in terms of consequence of their actions upon the seventh unborn generation. Contemporary life is geared to the length of political office.

~ Ghillean Prance

Trustees of creation

Make us trustees of your creation, Lord; defending it from exploitation, pollution, war; enjoying its fruits and gladly sharing with others. Amen

~ Ian M. Fraser

God bless tomatoes

God bless imperfect, garden-grown tomatoes
clean of herbicides and pesticides
and residues

God bless tomatoes
that taste of summer sun and
little children eat like apples

God bless carrots
of a strong colour

God bless good, rooted leeks

God bless freshly picked herbs of a pleasing odour
(and a goodly, Godly fragrance)

God bless lettuce that snails and slugs have kissed

God bless shiny green peppers,
beautiful inside as
High Gothic cathedrals

God bless radishes and beetroot and

potatoes caked with dirt

God bless dirt

(creased deep in the palms of hands and
stuck underneath fingernails)

God bless gardens and greenhouses and
next door neighbours who step out to shoot the breeze

God bless the cycles of seasons and
food we know the origins of

Help us to remember where we come from, God,
and to consider where on earth we are going.
Amen

~ *Neil Paynter*

(Tomatoes were the world's first genetically modified crop)

Global garden

In Guinea Bissau people scratch a living from tired earth
cash cropping for overfed northern markets.
In Somalia people carry muddy water for miles over arid desert tracks.
In Eritrea people pick over the bones of long dead stock
for bitter herbs.

The closest I came
to taking responsibility
for what I ate

was hand picking
apples
from the shelves
of out of town
superstores.
Then I made a garden.

In my garden,
I dig till my back aches and my fingers blister,
I wage war against the weather and weeds,
I compete with pests and pigeons,
I experience
success
and failure
in equal measure
not exactly famine
not exactly Eritrea
but maybe
just maybe
it brings me a
little closer
to an understanding
of what is
and what is not
important.

~ *Pete Anderson*

A 93-year-old woman talking about apples

'In ancient times we used to get all types of apples. We used to get Thamey Sweets, St Lawrence, crabs, russets, candy-striped, sheep's nose. Like a sheep's nose, yes. Sort of tapered. My mother would bake Thamey Sweets – and the skin would shine. So sweet you didn't need sugar. You just left the stem on and added cloves. A squatty kind of apple. God, the smell when they're baking,' said the old woman, and closed her eyes. Like it suddenly all came back to her. On a wave.

Prayer

Thank you God,
for the wisdom of 93-year-old women:
food for thought.

Thank you for apples. For Thamey Sweet apples,
St Lawrence apples, crab apples,
russet apples, candy-striped apples,
sheep's nose apples …

For the precious and amazing
diversity of your world.

May we never take that wealth for granted.
May we work to guard and secure it.
May we be full of wonder.

In the name of the One God:
the One God of many apples.
Amen

~ Neil Paynter

Prayers and responses

For rain and sun and insects to pollinate crops; for farmers who work with nature and preserve the beauty and diversity of God's creation; and for wild creatures which enjoy the harvest of berries, nuts, grains and seeds.

ALL: We give thanks, O God.

For the soil, rich and precious, home to countless living creatures which maintain fertility and give us food and life.

ALL: We give thanks, O God.

For growing awareness that we all depend on the earth for our daily food and fuel; and for the increasing numbers of people who want to eat local food and have closer links with food producers.

ALL: We give thanks, O God.

For wisdom to live in ways that will slow down climate change and keep the rains falling in their due season.

ALL: O Lord hear our prayer.

For caution in manipulating the building blocks of life in transferring genes between species.

ALL: O Lord hear our prayer.

For grace to recognise we are part of God's creation with responsibilities to care for God's earth and our fellow creatures, including farm animals both during their lives and in their deaths at abattoirs.

ALL: O Lord hear our prayer.

Bring peace to the killing fields of war, turn scorched earth to green, so that people can sow their seeds and harvest their crops and live in harmony with their neighbours.

ALL: Lord, send forth your Spirit.

Bring justice to those crushed by debt, forced to grow cash crops for us to consume, tempted to waste fertile land growing drugs and tobacco and denied access to land for growing their own food.

ALL: Lord, send forth your Spirit.

Send us out into the world, in service to God's creatures, as disciples of Jesus who blessed bread and wine at the Last Supper – bread which earth has given and human hands have made, and wine, fruit of the vine and work of human hands.

ALL: Lord, send forth your Spirit.

~ Christian Ecology Link

A new green dawn

God wisely chose
the colour green –
for shade of forests and grass.
The rice also of the East
and the wheat of the West
in youth is green

before turning to harvest.
Green is the ocean
under cloud-swept skies,
and all this colour
softly rests upon human eyes.

But suddenly
the green is fading.
The forests black with scorching fire;
the land eroded, turning to dust;
the lakes lying still and dead
with acid rain.
Fish die, birds fall from the sky,
and precious species, plant and beast
are gone
save in natural history books.

Lord, teach us
to touch your world
with more delicate hands.
Contain our greed,
and stir respect,
and open our eyes
to see all things as sacred –
all things as yours.
Bring us to a new green dawn.

~ L. David Levison

You bless us in the earth

O God, you bless us in the earth
and all that nourishes and sustains our bodies;
bless us too with that spirit of gratitude
which shows itself in the way
we care for the earth and its fruits;
through Jesus Christ our Lord.

~ Christian Aid

Windy, wet evening

On this windy, wet evening,
thanks Lord
for this
absolutely wonderful glass
of wine
and for its reminder
of your good earth
and soft rain
and glorious sunshine.

~ Peter Millar

Eat and enjoy

Food is ready;
people are gathered;
our earth's good things
are for sharing.
Come, eat and enjoy.

~ Joy Mead

Closing prayer

Our great Creator,
you have created all
in beauty and truth –
the blue skies of summer,
the green grass of spring,
the colours of autumn,
the soft snows of winter.

You created all in goodness.
Help us to live in kindness and gentleness.
Help us to share your peace
with each other and with
all the world.

~ Joyce Carlson

Readings:

Genesis 1:26–31
Job 12:7–10
Psalm 8
Psalm 104
Isaiah 24:4–6
Romans 8:18–25
Colossians 1:15–17

Seedtime,
Harvest,
FEASTING

The total Bread of Life

Some of us in the [Iona] community believe that it is no accident that brought us to the centre of the old Celtic tradition. For the first missionaries who went out from there carried not only a book, a bell and a staff. Each also carried a bag of seed. Christ was the total Bread of Life. May Iona become an ecumenical centre of Bread politics?

~ George MacLeod

To Christ the seed

To Christ the seed;
to Christ the sheaves:
so into God's barns
may we all be brought.

To Christ the sea;
to Christ the fish:
so into God's nets
may we all be caught.

From birth to growth,
from growth to age
may your two arms, O Christ,
fold us around.

From age to death,
from death to new birth
in the palace of grace
may we be found.

~ *Irish traditional*

The miracle of seed

For the miracle of seed
  energy of harvest
  concentration of milling
  warmth of baking
  joy of eating and sharing
we are thankful.

~ *Joy Mead*

Gift of life

For the lives of all who planted, watered and harvested
to provide the food before us,
and for your gift of life within the seed,
we give thanks, Creator God.

~ *Maureen Edwards*

Food as power

During the celebration in 1980 of the first anniversary of the Nicaraguan revolution, I stayed in Managua with Xabier Gorostiaga. He had been a William Paton Fellow in Selly Oak Colleges in Birmingham and was now the new economics supremo. He forecast then, yes over twenty years ago, that the giant multinationals would concentrate on controlling the world market in seeds. That way lay global power. That way lay a challenge to God's ownership of the earth and a contradiction of Paul's dictum: 'It is for freedom that Christ set us free' (Galat. 5:1). It is surely obscene to try to control that market by removing germination quality from seeds! Mozambique has known both sides of the food-as-power coin. The response to its plight gave evidence of a concerned world community. Will such concern persist beyond the food aid point, to help restore land to its fruitfulness?

~ Ian M. Fraser

For bread to share

For bread to share
today
and seeds to save
for tomorrow
we are thankful.

~ Joy Mead

Shadow of hunger

Living God,
our strength and help.
We turn to you in our distress.
May the spirit of compassion
comfort and protect your people.

In the parched land and failed harvests
we see you hungry.
May the shadow of that hunger
be broken by the light of your hope.

In our hearts we hold a vision
of a better world.
May we, by our actions,
bear witness to your love.

Amen

~ Linda Jones/CAFOD

Prayer for Southern Africa

To the countries where food is scarce,
mercy Lord, while there is still time.
To the countries where crops have failed,
rescue Lord, while there is time.
To countries where people are fearful,
security Lord, while there is time.

In the countries where we have plenty,
set our hearts on sharing this time.
In countries where we feel in control,
set our minds on justice at this time.
In countries where we forget those in need,
set our prayers on Africa at this time.

Amen

~ *Peter Graystone/Christian Aid*

A prayer from Sudan

Give life to the grass
by sending us rain.
Give life to our earth
by sending us rain.
Give life to our crops
by sending us rain.
Give life to our children
by sending us rain.

~ *From Christian Aid*

Life is a feast

Lord, I thank you for the food you have set before me.
Living as I do, life is a feast;
but I remember that for others life is a famine.

~ *The Church of Scotland*

Forgive us

Forgive us, Lord Jesus,
for grain mountains and milk lakes while stomachs are empty.
Forgive us for political and economic systems
which depend on the weak getting weaker and
the rich possessing the earth.
As we share this meal let us remember ...

~ David Jenkins/United Reformed Church prayerbook

If the poor didn't plant ...

If the poor didn't plant
what would the rich do?
They have money in their pockets
but that doesn't produce food.
The person who walks barefoot
is the one who produces
in order to see Brazil grow.

~ Jose Costa Leita/CAFOD

Shared by all

In our time, Dives and Lazarus are hemispheres as well as groupings within countries. The parable has to do with the debt crisis, with Western banks prospering while Third World countries live on crumbs. Third World countries certainly over-reached themselves in their borrowing but their plight is not simply of their own making. Western bankers hold responsibility for pushing hot money towards them; governments are responsible for raising interest rates and making the borrowing countries pay the piper: the IMF is responsible for imposing conditions which fall hardest on the poor. It is Dives' power position which ensures Lazarus's abject condition …

What we do not get in the parable is a condemnation of wealth as such. Lazarus is depicted resting in Abraham's bosom, and we have no evidence that Abraham in his life was short of a penny or two. What contradicts God's Kingdom of Love is where one human being is lording it and stuffing himself, while another human being is languishing in abject misery. Just as was the case in 1 Cor. 11, where 'each of you takes his own supper, and one goes hungry and another has too much to drink', the blasphemy is in refusing to see that sharing in Christ implies sharing with one another. In discerning what is sufficiency, we are faced with an ongoing task – because in the glimpses we get in the Bible, sufficiency may be a belt-tightener or a belt-buster. As Filipino landworkers when they met with Ed de la Torre for a Mass realised, the little bits of rice cake and little sips of wine brought home the message that to be in Christ means sharing. The sharing is not to be postponed in times of great scarcity, and the weak and young and old are to get the same portion as the strong; but also, in times of abundance, all can stuff themselves! The picture of God's creation in the Garden of Eden story is one of abundance. The promise is of the feast of wine to the lees and fat things full of marrow. The anticipated city of God is furnished with trees which provide fruit every month of the year. The sufficiency which

God offers is a 'pressed down running over' sufficiency – when what is provided for all is shared by all, but not before that ...

~ *Ian M. Fraser*

Grace

Jesus said: 'My food is to do the will of the
one who sent me.'

We thank you, God of creation,
for the food which nourishes bodies.
Give us also that food which compels us to
    do your will
and to share the fruits of creation among all;
through Jesus Christ our Lord.

~ *Christian Aid*

Harvest prayer

Loving Creator God,
at harvest time we gaze in wonder
at the splendour of your creation.
We see a banquet spread before us,
rich carpeted fields of yellowing grain
and overflowing baskets of ripe fruit.
We see a banquet prepared for all peoples
of fine wines and rich food
a generous feast for all to share.

Help us to learn from your generosity
how to share our bread with the hungry
and open our hearts to the poor,
to commit ourselves to preparing
a banquet for all peoples
a generous feast for all to share

~ *Linda Jones/CAFOD*

From earth and sky

From the earth the grain, the gift of life to feed us.
From the sky the rain, bring blessings on our bread.

The earth and water, fire and air, the gift of life to feed us.
The earth and water, fire and air, bring blessings on our bread.

~ *Jenny Joyce and Alan Whear*

Sung to the tune of La Morrisque: an old morris tune

Blessing of the cheese and olives

Sanctify this milk that has been pressed into cheese, and press us
together in charity. Grant that this fruit of the olive-tree may never
lose its savour; for the olive is a symbol of abundance which,
at your bidding, flowed from the tree and is there for those who
trust you.

~ *Greece, 2nd or 3rd century*

Prayer of praise and thanksgiving

As we celebrate our plenty
and give thanks for our food,
Father we praise you
for all you have done and for all you have given.

For shelves that are laden and cupboards that are full.
For food available, varied, and affordable.
For taste and for flavour,
for a healthy appetite
and the means to satisfy it.
For all that is symbolised in this Harvest Service
Creator and Sustainer of all,
we thank and praise you.

For Provider and Producer,
God and farmer working together in harmony.
For all in the food chain,
from field to factory,
retailer to consumer,
each one depending on the others,
Creator and Sustainer of all,
we thank and praise you.

For our countryside
fertile, diverse and beautiful,
supplying so much of what we need;
our food, our water,
crops for industry, energy and medicine.

Source of our leisure, relaxation and renewal.
Creator and Sustainer of all,
we thank and praise you.
Amen

~ *Arthur Rank Centre*

Prayer of intercession

We pray for
those whose lives are caught up with your creation,
and who work with you in tending and nurturing it.
Those who even now suffer as a result of the crisis in the countryside.
Those afraid for their future,
those struggling to survive,
all whose livelihood and existence is under threat.

May they know your presence and be conscious of the help that you bring.
Through both may they find hope for their future.
For we ask it in Jesus' name.
Amen

~ *Arthur Rank Centre*

The earth and all its fullness

God, teach us that the earth and all its fullness is yours,
    the world and those who dwell in it.
Remind us that your Son too
    enjoyed the fruits of harvest in Galilee.
And join us now as we celebrate your good gifts together.
Call us yet again to safeguard the gift of life,
    now and for ever.
Amen

~ *Christian Ecology Link*

God of the seed-time

God of the seed-time and the harvest,
the making and the baking
the breaking and the sharing
may food, friendship and thankfulness
nourish our compassion
and give energy to our protest
so that time will come
when all share in the feasting
and the fun.

~ *Joy Mead*

Yours is the Moon, yours is the Sun

Yours is the Moon, yours is the Sun,
Yours is the seed time, the harvest and rain.
You give us food, opening your hand,
great son of Mary of God's own heart.
Come to us now, son of the Pure,
Son of the Most High, come join in our feast,
Bless now our food, bless now our hearth,
bless now the people who call on you.

~ John Newton, Worth Abbey Lay Community

Lord of the Feast

Lord of the Feast, we ask your blessing on
those who produced this food
those who provided this food
those who prepared this food
and we who enjoy this food.

~ Alix Brown

From furrow dark

Round for two voices

From fur-row dark in light-filled air, Green leaves grow-ing. In all we eat from light we feed! Ri-pened in sun's glow-ing, The fruits of earth to live we need. Gra-ti-tude show-ing.

~ *Music & words: C A Lindenberg, Camphill Community*
From Fran Clay, Loch Arthur Community

From you the grain

Here we are gathered, here we have come.
Bless us, O God, and bless these your gifts.
Yours is the sun, yours is the rain,
ripening the grain and giving it growth.
From you the grain, from you the grape
from you the growth of the fairest of gifts.
Here you have called us, here we have come.
Bless us, O God, and bless these your gifts.

~ John Newton, Worth Abbey Lay Community

God, the promise of life

God, the promise of life
in magical, rain-washed apples
and glowing, sunlit strawberries;
in brown, crusty bread,
soft at its heart;
in broad beans and cabbages
as green as tomorrow;
in cheese that crumbles on the tongue
and tastes of dew damp fields;
in the sweet floweriness of honey
and the wonderful harmony of herbs,
may we be ever thankful
for the variety of food
and the creativity of cooks.

~ Joy Mead

A poem ...

I don't like onion
I don't like the taste
and when I was young
I was in hospital
the nurse said
I had to eat it
I was five or
six years old
I was in hospital
for epilepsy

I like

liver
bacon
sausages
beans
fish
chips
potatoes
cauliflower
green peas
green beans
brussels
spring greens
mash
roast potatoes

strawberries
fruit pies
baked apple

~ ATD Fourth World family member

... and a grace

Sausages
beans
chips
and ice-cream,
it can't get
much better than this,
can it God?

~ Ruth Burgess

The earth is the Lord's

Lord, your hands have formed this world,
every part is shaped by you –
water tumbling over rocks, air and sunlight:
each day's signs that you make all things new.

Yours the soil that holds the seed,
you give warmth and moisture too.
Sprouting blossoms, crops and buds, trees and plants:
the season's signs that you make all things new.

Sweet potatoes fill our bags,
when the garden yields its due.

Chickens run and pigs grow plump, children too:
your bounty's signs that you make all things new.

We search out new ground to weed,
even mountain fields will do.
You uproot the toughest sins from our souls:
both steward signs that you make all things new.

Like a mat you roll out land,
space to build, for us and you
earthly homes and, better still, homes for Christ:
the truest sign that you make all things new.

~ *From The Philippines, Ramon and Sario Oliano, paraphrase James Minchin*

A substantial faith

Give us a substantial faith.
Even before we call, you are answering
      and you are hearing us right now.
We have been quickened,
nothing delays our rejoicing.
We have been made clean,
a right spirit now invades our minds
and courses through our veins.
We are strong, on firmest ground, and free.
We have come again to feasting and festivities
      radiant with new clothing.
      Smothered with your kiss of peace.

~George MacLeod

Blessing of loaves, blessing of fish

Bless - ing of loaves, bless - ing of fish;

thou - sands are fed; a gift of God.

King of that feast, lord of this fare,

~ Text & music: da Noust

Readings:

Genesis 8:22
Deuteronomy 8:7–10
Haggai 1:5–11
Mark 4:26–32
Luke 14:15–24
James 1:18
Revelation 19:9

Readings
from the BIBLE

Some verses from the Psalms

Psalm 8 (vv. 1, 6, 7, 8, 9)

Wonderful God, Creator, the whole earth declares your greatness.

You share with us responsibility to care for sheep and cattle, wild things, birds and fish, everything that lives in the sea: to work with you, within creation.

Wonderful God, Creator, the whole earth declares your greatness.

Psalm 23 (vv. 1, 6)

You are my shepherd, O God; I need nothing more.

Goodness and kindness unfailing will follow me all my days.
I shall make my home in the house of God for as long as I shall live.

Psalm 65 (vv. 9, 10, 11, 12, 13)

You care for the earth and water it;
you fill it with riches, it streams with water;
you prepare the earth to give grain to its people.

You soak the furrows and level the ridges;
you soften the ground with rain
and bless the land with growth.

You crown the year with riches,
and all that you touch comes alive:
the untilled pastures yield crops,
the hills are wreathed in joy.

The meadows are clothed with sheep
and the valleys decked with grain,
so that with shouts of delight
everything breaks into song. Amen

Psalm 104 (vv. 13, 14, 15, 24, 27, 28)

From your dwelling you water the hills
and the earth drinks its fill of your gift.

For cattle you make the grass grow,
and for people the plants they need
to bring forth food from the earth
and wine to gladden their hearts.

How countless are your works, O God;
all of them made so wisely;
a world teeming with creatures!

All of them look to you
to give them food in due season.
You give and they gather;
you open your hand and they have their fill.

~ Iona Abbey Worship Book

More verses from the Psalms and other Bible readings:

Psalm 22:26
Psalm 68:19
Psalm 78:23–29
Psalm 92:1–4
Psalm 106:1
Psalm 128:1–2
Psalm 145:15–16

Exodus 23:25
1 Chronicles 29:13
Proverbs 15:17
John 6:11–14
1 Corinthians 10:31
1 Thessalonians: 5:16–18
1 Timothy 6:17

From different
TRADITIONS

ISLAM

Prayer before a meal

'B' ism Allah ArRahman ARRahim'

'In the name of Allah, The Beneficent, The Merciful'

~ From the Moslem Council of Britain

Prayer after a meal

Ramadan Kareem

The meal must be ready exactly as the sun disappears over the horizon, easily seen from Qasmiyeh as it dips below the Mediterranean, and then we wait for the call from the mosque. One sees people hurrying from house to house with dishes of food for friends and neighbours, for nobody must go without, for it is Ramadan Kareem, best translated, I think, as generous. There is a favourite Ramadan prayer:

For I have done my duty in hospitality to every guest,
I am Thy guest, let my guest portion this night be Paradise.

~ Runa Mackay

BAHÁ'Í

In the Bahá'í faith there is no real concept of saying grace. Although there are many wonderful prayers in the Bahá'í scriptures, there is really no concept of a grace or a prayer that is said before or after meals. Each nineteen days Bahá'í communities celebrate the Nineteen-day feast – a spiritual feast 'to bind hearts together' (Baha'u'llah). During this time, community members come together to worship, share music, food and fellowship, and to discuss practical matters.

~ Bahá'í Community/Ed.

Prayer

Lord! Pitiful are we, grant us Thy favour; poor, bestow upon us a share from the ocean of Thy wealth; needy, do Thou satisfy us; abased, give us Thy glory. The fowls of the air and the beasts of the field receive their meat each day from Thee, and all beings partake of Thy care and loving-kindness.

Deprive not this feeble one of Thy wondrous grace and vouchsafe by Thy might unto this helpless soul Thy bounty.

Give us our daily bread, and grant Thine increase in the necessities of life, that we may be dependent on none other but Thee, may commune wholly with Thee, may walk in Thy ways and declare Thy mysteries. Thou art the Almighty and the Loving and the Provider of all mankind.

~ 'Abdu'l Bahá
  From Bahá'í Community of the UK

JUDAISM

Jesus's countrymen lived much closer to nature than do most of us today. They were nearer to the good earth and the wonder of the sprouting seed buried in the soil: the growth of the green blades and the ripening of the grain under the sun. No Jewish father would dream of eating a meal with his family without first giving God thanks: and this is the lovely prayer they used for giving thanks before eating in Jesus's days:

Prayer

We give thanks to Thee, Lord God, King of the Universe, who makest bread to come out of the earth.

~ The Very Rev. Dr George Reid

HINDUISM

Brahman Himself is the oblation; Brahman Himself is whatever constitute the oblation; by Brahman Himself is the oblation poured into the fire of Brahman; Brahman shall truly be reached by him who always sees Brahman in all actions.

~ The Bhagavad Gita IV, 24

BUDDHISM

Four Gathas

Serving food

In this food
I see clearly the presence
of the entire universe
supporting my existence.

Contemplating your food

This plate of food,
so fragrant and appetising,
also contains much suffering.

Beginning to eat

With the first taste, I promise to offer joy.
With the second, I promise to help relieve the suffering of others.
With the third, I promise to see others' joy as my own.
With the fourth, I promise to learn the way of non-attachment
and equanimity.

Finishing your meal

The plate is empty.
My hunger is satisfied.
I vow to live
for the benefit of all beings.

~ Thich Nhat Hanh, Plum Village, France

SIKHISM

Prayer

Our grateful thanks to Him who gives us the food we eat.

~ Prayer from The Network of Sikh Organisations

JAINISM

In Jainism, food is not seen as the gift of a superior being but as the result of one's karma. Jains strive to be free of all karmas and to be pure souls. When praying Jains especially remember their spiritual teachers who walk the path that leads to purity.

Although some Jains recite mantras or stanzas before meals, there is no particular prayer which Jains say before eating. Before a meal, some Jains wait a moment in case a saint or someone who is hungry comes to their door. If someone comes, they will provide food to him/her first. After that, before they start to take food, they recite the Navkär (Namokar) Mantra three times.

Navkär (Namokar) Mantra

I bow down to Arihantas who have attained perfect knowledge and are supreme teachers,

I bow down to Siddhas who are pure souls and liberated from this world.

I bow down to Ächäryas who are the supreme spiritual teachers and pass on the teachings of Arihanta,

I bow down to Upädhyäyas who are also spiritual teachers and teach the message of Arihanta to other spiritual teachers,

I bow down to Sädhus and Sädhvis who are the ordinary spiritual teachers and also pass on the teachings of Arihanta.

These obeisances destroy all the impurities.
Amongst all the auspicious mantras,
this Navkär Mantra is the most auspicious.

~ From Jainworld

162   Blessed Be Our Table

TAOISM

The courts are polished and decorated,
while the fields are untilled,
and the granaries are empty.
People wear fine clothes
to adorn their external appearance.
They carry sharp swords at their sides
and worship might rather than righteousness.
They know only to make merry
by indulging in food and drink.
They crave to possess more riches
than they could ever use.

This is the committing of robbery
and is not the Universal Integral Way of natural life.

~ Lao Tzu

CONFUCIANISM

The Master said: 'Even in the midst of eating coarse rice and drinking water and using a bent arm for a pillow happiness is surely to be found; riches and honours acquired by unrighteous means are to me like the floating clouds.'

~ Confucius

Creator, Son
& HOLY SPIRIT

God's power in weakness

God,
who created all of us
in the variety of our human nature,
we give ourselves to love you
as you have loved us.

Jesus our Lord,
showing God's power in weakness,
compassionate friend,
may we accept and welcome each other,
as we are accepted in you.

Holy Spirit,
dwelling in each of us,
we praise you for joining us together
in bonds of love and truth.
Give us your healing grace
to live together in fellowship
and serve each other in peace and joy.

So may your kingdom come.

Amen

~ da *Noust*

A trinity of graces

Loving Creator God,

We thank you for this beautiful earth from which our food comes.
We thank you for the long chain of people who grow, harvest
and transport it,
who sell, buy and prepare it,
and for those who now serve, share and eat it.

Bless the world and all its people, ourselves and this food,
to bring life and harmony
within your whole creation.

We ask it for your love's sake.

Amen

Lord Jesus,

You cradled ordinary bread in your hands, blessed and shared it.
You said, 'This is my body.'

Bless this food which we are about to eat.
May we receive it with reverence and thankful hearts.
May we share with all your children
in openness, love and generosity.

Amen

Holy Spirit,

You moved over the earth at its creation.
You brought order out of chaos and life out of randomness.

Help us to cherish this beautiful, fragile world from which our life comes, and to seek justice for the many vulnerable people who work to produce food for our tables.

Bless this food, the world and its people, that we may live as you intended, in harmony with creation and with thankful hearts and lives.

Amen

~ Frances Hawkey

Bless all our sharing

We share food, wine (tea, coffee, whatever!) and conversation
as followers of Jesus.
Father, thanks for the work of your children all over the world
which has brought these good things to our table.
Jesus, truly one of us, bless all our sharing,
Holy Spirit, fill our eating, drinking and speaking with love for God
and for each other.

~ Ian Cowie

The Maker's blessing be upon the food

The Maker's blessing be upon the food,
the Christ's blessing be upon each one,
the Spirit's blessing weave through
words and listening;
taste and digesting.
God's blessing be upon this meal.

~ *Chris Polhill*

Food from God's good earth

Food from God's good earth
and love kindled by His spirit,
these we share together in joy,
in the Name of Christ, the Living Bread.

~ *Ian Cowie*

A tea-time grace from Sri Lanka

Even as the water falls on dry tea leaves
and brings out their flavour,
so may your spirit fall on us and renew us,
so that we may bring refreshment and joy to others.

~ *Kithu Sevena, Sri Lanka*
  From Christian Aid

Kirisuto no heiwa ga

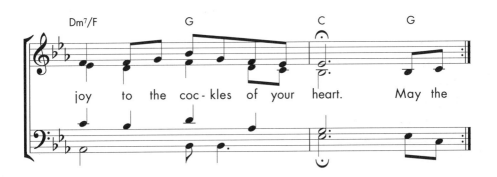

Kirisuto no heiwa ga (May the breath of God) –
May the breath of God be in you,
may the fire of love you knew from the start
and the peace of the one who makes new
bring you joy to the cockles of your heart.

Ki-ri-su-to no hei-wa ga
Wa-ta-si-ta-chi no ko-ko-ro no
Su-mi-zu-mi-i-ni ma-a-de
yu-ki-wa-ta-ri-ma-su-yo-o-ni

May the peace of Christ fill our hearts.

~ *Text & music: Fr Izumi Shiota. Trans & Arr: da Noust.*

The Japanese original has a minim and crochet in place of the dotted minim at the end of the first line.

Readings:

Luke 1:35
John 20:22
Acts 1:7–9
Acts 10:38
2 Corinthians 13:14
Ephesians 1:3–14
Ephesians 2:19–22

God of
COMMUNITY

Community jubilee

Opening our heartache, the anguish of our lives,
doubts and fears depress us, and faith our words belie;
Hunting for your waymarks, in footprints of our lives,
called to tell our story, and see a new hope rise:

Come, Spirit of yearning, you welcome all we despise,
come, Spirit of glory, from you our hopes arise;
come, coming through water, erupting Spirit of joy,
O, Spirit of freedom, our debts of hate destroy.

~ da *Noust*
  Tune: Alabanza, Puerto Rico[9]

God of community

God of community –
God of the here and now –
thank you for gathering us
under one roof
and round many tables.
Thank you for giving us
a healthy hunger
and good food.

~ *Jan Sutch Pickard*

Living in community

Living in community was not easy. The things which caused offence were not differences in theology or ecclesiastical practice, but matters such as snoring and eating habits.

'We were a splendid community,' said George, 'except at meal times!' …

~ *Ron Ferguson*

Thank you for our day

Thank you for our day,
and sorry for times that were hard,
Please help us all to live in peace and love.

~ *da Noust*
  Sung to the adapted tune of 'Compliment'[10], *Wild Goose Resource Group.*

Porridge and milk

Porridge and milk make community,
bringing out flavours in one another.
May we so make community.
Amen

~ *Ian M. Fraser*

An Iona grace

For blue sky, blue sea,
and the wonderfully appetising smell
of homemade bread and soup
which we are about to share,
we thank you, living, loving God.
Amen

~ Sheila Woodcock

Iona grace 2

For good food lovingly prepared,
and friends old and new to share it with,
thank you God
Amen

~ Sheila Woodcock

Saying grace

'One of the things I appreciated most about community life was saying grace before meals. I don't come from a religious background, and being grateful for food, for friends, for a warm, safe place to sleep, for the day – for all the "basics" in life – opens you up to the political, I think. You become more aware, and concerned that others have the basics of life, too – nutritious food, clean water, free speech, basic human rights.'

~ A volunteer with the Iona Community on Iona

For those without food

God, thank you for this beautiful meal
and for beautiful friends to share it with.
We think of those who are without food and love in their lives.
May this food give us the strength to work for justice and peace
in the community of your world.
Amen

~ Neil Paynter

Storms and rainbows

For work and worship
prayer and action
being and doing

for sharing stories and for sharing beauty beyond words
for long walks alone and for pilgrimages together
for the sound of the ferry and for the echo of church bells
for quiet time and for the wild dance of the spirit
for storms that pass and for rainbows
for daffodils in bloom and for a night full of stars ...

For all of these things and
for all of the ways these things
feed into each other.
For this life-giving food and
for the varied food of life.
For all of the ways you nourish us,
loving God, we praise you.
Amen

~ Neil Paynter

God is great

God is   great,_____   I tell you God is great.

God is great, I tell you God is great
God is good, I tell you God is good
God is hope, I tell you God is hope
God is peace, I tell you God is peace
God is joy, I tell you God is joy
God is love ...

~ African – source unknown

Volunteers from Africa brought this song to Iona, and taught it to a group of us one night in the old coffeehouse. We often had nights like that on Iona. Nights when volunteers from different continents and countries – Africa, Pakistan, Australia, North America, Mexico – would get together and share music, food and stories.

Since Columba's time, Iona has been a crossroads. It still is.

The first bar is meant to be sung by a cantor, with a group answering with the second bar. Harmonies might be improvised. The words 'God is great/God is good' might be adapted and expanded upon. For example:

> *God is great,*
> *God is good,*
> *God is hope,*
> *God is peace,*
> *God is joy,*
> *God is love ...*

We used this song a couple of times in the Abbey and, on occasion, before and after meals. (Ed.)

An October grace

Creator God, who brings the storm and calm and is present in each,
we give you thanks for the raging wind and crashing waves,
as we are held here in safety with shelter and friends and food to share.

We pray for those travelling on the seas –
keep them safe, O God.
For those whose storms are homelessness and hunger,
and who travel the rough seas of loneliness and pain,
may they know your peace.

May our prayers be turned to action
and our thoughts be turned to compassion.
Amen

~ Rachel McCann, Camas, October 2001

Originally quarry workers' cottages, then a salmon fishing station, the Camas Centre on the Isle of Mull is run by a staff group with specialist skills, helped by several volunteers. Young people from the city and elsewhere, and other groups too, come to Camas for an adventure holiday with outdoor opportunities for canoeing, walking, swimming and camping, a visit to Iona, and the experience of exploring issues, building relationships, and facing new challenges through living and working in community. [11]

Who is that knocking at my door?

Revelation 3:20

The Open Door Community is a residential Christian community in downtown Atlanta, at 910 Ponce de Leon Avenue, about a mile and a quarter from the Fox Theatre on Peachtree. A group of some thirty of us live together in an old apartment building that is owned by the Open Door Community and by the Greater Atlanta Presbytery, which consists of all its supporting churches. In those rooms, within those walls, we struggle together to lead a life of obedience and servanthood to the call and gift of Jesus Christ in our lives.

We are a community of diversity – a lot of different kind of folk coming to live together: joyful and grumpy, short and tall, mainline and marginalised, black and white and brown, formally educated and street – or prison – educated, artists, poets, singers, crossbearers, brothers and sisters. Even our grumpy ones laugh a lot. We've all been mighty hungry, and we are learning how to eat together. Recently we were honoured to open our door to a knock, a knock to which we have listened several times over the last years, and in came a man called Amos Jones. He is also an embodiment of Jesus Christ. When we listen and open the door, Jesus comes in and lives with us; he eats with us, and we eat with him. Amos has cancer in both of his legs, and it is spreading. Amos has AIDS, and it is full-blown. Amos has come to us from one of the holy places in this city – Grady Memorial Hospital – one of the most important institutions for those who are poor and marginalised. I plead for your support and help for Grady Memorial Hospital. It is a place under attack.

We are a community that lives with Amos, and Amos lives with us. We live with Jesus, and Jesus lives with us. We're a community that is black and white; we are strong and weak; some of us are highly educated, and some of us are unable to read. We have women and we have men. Sometimes we have children – not all the time. We have a number of us who are ageing. And we are young people. We have people whose hope and energy is fierce and feisty and ready. And we have people who are despairing, who think America doesn't give a damn about the poor, who think the church has turned its back, who think that Jesus doesn't knock on the door, but that Jesus is busy, off doing something else – like playing golf – and has forgotten about the cry of the prisoner, or the hunger of the hungry. So we are shaped by the goodness of God, by the cross of Jesus Christ, to live a life in community with diversity.

We are a community of worship. Each morning at 5.50 those journeying to the wonderful Butler Street CME Church to feed two hundred men and women and a few children gather in a circle to hear the Word. After serving the awesome breakfast of coffee, cheese grits, a boiled egg, three-quarters of an orange, and a multivitamin we sweep and mop the floors. We clean the toilets and lavatories. We pick up trash and sweep the sidewalk in front of the church and along the sidewalk on Coca Cola Place. Then we sit for our own breakfast. 'The grits have God in them,' Leo promises us! We re-read the scripture lesson, and then reflect on the morning's activities. Did you see Jesus today? How was our hospitality and welcome? What public policies must be changed to harness the devil and roll away the stone from the tomb of Christ? Who are the leaders, and what are the values that create and sustain hunger in the midst of plenty? Then we beg Yahweh to get us going toward the wilderness, and head home to 910.

Every day we feed hundreds of people, and after our soup kitchen at 910 we clean up. Then we gather, before we eat, for a time of listening and remembering those who have knocked on our door. We read the word of God, reflect, and pray. On Sunday afternoon at 5.00 pm we have a worship service with the Eucharist followed by a yummy meal prepared by Adolphus or Leo. Four times each year while on retreat at Dayspring – a farm near Ellijay, Georgia, several hours north of Atlanta – we celebrate the sacrament of foot washing. We are 'fools for Christ and wish we were more so', Dorothy Day teaches us as she sits amid the clouds as a witness ...

~ Ed Loring, The Open Door Community, Atlanta, USA

A cup of rice, a cup of wheat

4-part round

A cup of rice, a cup of wheat, for ev - 'ry

hun - gry child in need, and more we ask, O God a -

-bove, for ev - 'ry child a home with love.

~ Carl Maendel & Marlys Swinger, from the Bruderhof Community

The Bruderhof is an international community movement rooted in Anabaptist and early Christian traditions, committed to non-violence, justice and fellow-ship, based on Christ's Sermon on the Mount.

Good friends

For good food and good friends, thank you Lord.
Amen

~ From L'Arche Inverness, original source unknown

This grace was a favourite of Ian Cameron, 1926–2000, who was the first person with a learning disability welcomed to L'Arche Inverness, and who was also a co-founder of the community.

To hear his heartbeat

Abba, father,
into your hands we commend our spirit
and our thirst.

Create in us a community
who welcome weakness,
in covenant with Jesus.
You have given us, one to another;
may we stay close enough to hear his heartbeat.

~ da Noust
Tune: by Chemin Neuf Artemas

Chew on the gospels

Chew on the gospels,
let their word transform our lives,
let all we do be with God's breath inspired.
Listen to God,
obey the word of Jesus,
holding to love,
so learning to forgive.

Find help on the way of transfiguration,
trust in God, who hears our cry for bread.

~ Words and music: da Noust

The bread is not our food

4-part round

The bread is not our food. What feeds us in the
bread is God's e - ter - nal Word, is Spi - rit and is Life.

Text: Angelus Silesius. Music: Barry Graham, Loch Arthur Community.

Graces from the Ty Mam Duw Poor Clare Colettine Community, Wales

These graces are sung on one note with excursions and harmonies

O blessed Poverty
To those who love and embrace her she gives eternal riches.
    Therefore I tell you:
    Do not be anxious about your life,
    what you are to eat
    and what you are to drink,
    for your heavenly Father knows your needs.

O holy Poverty
to those who possess and desire her
God promises the kingdom of heaven.
    Seek first his kingdom
    and his righteousness
    and all these things shall be yours as well.

O God-centred poverty
whom our Lord Jesus Christ
embraced completely.

Blessed are you, O Lord our God,
and blessed is your holy and glorious name.
You fill the hungry with good things;
may your right hand bless this humble gift of love,
and may your works
praise you for ever and ever.
Amen

Giving thanks

He gives food to all living things
for his great love is without end.
To the God of heaven give thanks
for his great love is without end.
We give you thanks,
most high eternal God
living and true
with your Son,
our beloved Lord Jesus Christ,
and the Holy Spirit the comforter,
for ever and ever.
Amen

The above quotations on poverty are from the letters of St Clare; the thanks-giving prayer is from the writings of St Francis.

We are mendicant contemplatives and this is not just poetry. The cook goes to the alms table where the portresses put the food alms given in and uses what there is – sometimes she pops out half way through the morning to see if anything else has arrived that ought to be used immediately!

~ Ty Mam Duw Poor Clare Colettine Community

Ty Mam Duw is an enclosed contemplative community of Franciscan women who have given their lives to the Lord in love of him and for the needs of all his children.

Table prayers from the Irish tradition

Before the meal:

Son of God,
you shared the blessing of the loaves and fishes
with the five thousand.
May your blessing be upon us now and upon our sharing of this meal.

After the meal:

All praise to the King of Heaven,
all praise to our God,
all praise to Jesus Christ for this meal.
He has granted us food on earth;
may he also grant us eternal food in heaven.

~ Fr Vincent Madden, Mount Melleray Abbey

These prayers are used at Glenstal Abbey, a Benedictine monastery in County Limerick in the south-west region of Ireland. The Abbey, dedicated to Saints Joseph and Columba, is home to a community of monks who assemble in church four times a day for the Divine Office, and once a day for the concelebrated Mass. Benedictine worship emphasises beauty and harmony, celebrating God's presence, while it evokes a response of loving reverence in the monks. The activities of the community include a school for boys, a guest house, a farm and various publications of liturgical and spiritual interest.

A simple and colourful feast

Thank you Lord for this simple and colourful feast.
Nourish us by it so that we may serve you better.

~ *Stella Durand, member of Community of Aidan and Hilda*

Thankful hearts

We lift thankful hearts to you, O God. Teach us to accept
all you give us with gratitude and wonder and the impulse
to share generously.

~ *Stella Durand, member of Community of Aidan and Hilda*

The Community of Aidan and Hilda is a dispersed, ecumenical body of Christians who seek to create a Christian spirituality for today that renews the church and heals the land. It welcomes people of all backgrounds and countries who wish to be wholly available to the Holy Trinity, and to the way of Jesus as revealed to us in the Bible. In the earthing of that commitment members draw inspiration from Celtic saints such as Aidan and Hilda. Members follow a Way of Life, with a soul friend, based on a rhythm of prayer and study, simplicity, care for creation and mission. (From Healing the Land – Renewing the Church)

Du bist unser alles

Sung calmly and softly, the rhythm of the words fitting the flow of the music

Du bist unser alles,
unser Leben, unser Licht,
unser heil, unsere Speise,
unser Trank, unser Gott

You are our all, our life,
our light, our salvation,
our meal, our drink
our God!

~ *Text: St Columbanus © Bischof Prof. Dr Paul-Werner Scheele.*
Translation: Sr Mirjam Zahn & Music: Sr Adelheid Wenzelmann, both from
the Communität Christusbruderschaft.

The Communität Christusbruderschaft is a Protestant order within the Lutheran Church of Bavaria. The centre is situated in Selbitz, 130 km north-east of Nuremberg. Its members, men and women, have agreed to stay within a binding, life-long fellowship that is to be a witness for God.

From the Findhorn Community

Your attitude when you eat anything should be one of joy and pleasure and thanksgiving. You are to be constantly aware that all these gifts are Mine.

~ Eileen Caddy's guidance

The more food your body absorbs from the garden, the better. As you eat, try always to think of all those who have helped with the growing of the foodstuffs, the devas, the nature spirits, the angels; by doing this you are showing your recognition and appreciation for all that has been done to help the things grow there.

~ Eileen Caddy's guidance

Today the Findhorn Foundation is the central educational and organisational heart of a widely diverse community of several hundred people, spanning dozens of holistic businesses and initiatives all linked by a shared positive vision for humanity and the earth, and a commitment to the deep and practical non-doctrinal spirituality established in the Findhorn Community by it founders. (From the Findhorn Foundation website)

A Duncraig grace

The tendency here at Duncraig is the ad lib version of grace, dependent on who's at the table and what's on it. 'For these we give thanks ...' So, a Duncraig grace might go along the lines of:

God, you are great,
you give us sunshine and time to enjoy it,

new friends and good food and
you top it off with wine.

We are so fortunate and grateful to be loved by you.
Thank you God for all your provision, you are great.

PS God, we give special thanks for (*name of guest*) joining us.
Amen

I can't say it's ever been said just like that, verbatim, but as with all things in Duncraig, each is an original.

~ *Jenny McLellan*

(Duncraig is a Christian quiet house on the Isle of Iona)

Casa Ave Maria prayer

Danos corazones agradecidos, Padre y Madre Nuestro,
por todas tus bondades,
y haznos conscientes de las necesidades y los derechos de los démas.
Por Cristo Nuestro Señor.
Amen

Give us grateful hearts, our Father and Mother,
for all your good gifts,
and make us mindful of the needs and rights of others.
Through Christ our Lord.
Amen

~ *From Grant Gallup, Casa Ave Maria, Anglican guest house, Nicaragua*

Marion J. Hatchett's 'Commentary on the American Prayer Book' says that the source of this prayer, which has 'been in use for many years, is unknown. It entered the Prayer Book in 1928.'

We had copies of it printed and placed at each table setting here at the Casa for years, and then one day our friend, a Los Angeles missionary nurse here in Nicaragua, suggested we add 'Madre', and we did so; and another friend, a visitor from Grace Cathedral San Francisco, suggested we add 'rights' to the 'needs' of others, and so we did. When a few years ago we had the prayer fixed into tiles to repair the wall of the dining room, we therefore had an easily memorised prayer which was actually the result of organic growth. So, we have a prayer that combines the best of the old prayer, is gender inclusive, and recognises rights as well as needs in our aspirations.

At Casa Ave Maria we have for thirteen years (since I retired and moved here from Chicago) had free classes for neighbourhood youth, which have grown from English classes to classes also in dance, piano, guitar, recorder, marimba, and computers. We receive pilgrims from the USA and other countries (this is a guest house, too), introduce them gently to the realities of the Two Thirds World, and invite them to work in solidarity projects with the poor. We teach all our guests to pray bilingually!

~ Grant Gallup

A grace from the Indigenous Hospitality House

Gracious God,

We thank you for all your gifts to us; for this day and for these gifts of grain, of fruit, and meat. We thank you for all those whose hands have brought this good food to our table.

We remember the farmers who work long hours – may they work to keep the land fertile and healthy. We remember the truck-drivers who carry the produce around the country, and the workers in factories and shops – may they earn a fair wage in fair conditions.

We ask that you be with those who have little or no food to eat tonight. And we especially remember the indigenous people of this land – may your Spirit be with them as they struggle for justice and recognition of their rightful relationship with the land.

Finally we thank you for a place to come home to, and for the gift of each other.

May this food strengthen us to do your will.

Amen

This is a combination of bits and pieces that are commonly used in table graces at the Indigenous Hospitality House where I live. The Indigenous Hospitality House is a communal house in Melbourne that offers two rooms for indigenous families who have come from out of town to support a family member in hospital. The house is run by a small group of volunteers as part of their response to Christ. We are a mix of people from the Uniting Church in Australia, the Baptist Church, and the Quakers, and we even connect with the Little Sisters of Jesus.

Grace varies at our place at dinner time – from elements of the grace above, to Quaker grace (silence finished by 'Thanks friends').

~ Stephanie Tashkoff

A grace from Bethany – Jeremy's grace

All life is sacred – plant, animal, human.
All must eat to live and nourish one another.
So let us eat, consciously resolving by our life and actions
to honour those that died that we might live.

We ran a painting retreat, and the instructor/artist taught us this grace but didn't know the source, except that it came from 'friends of friends of friends ...' and that Jeremy was happy for it to be passed on. We always refer to it as 'Jeremy's grace'. We haven't heard it anywhere else. We use this one a lot, and we delight, somehow, in not knowing who 'Jeremy' is.

Walkers, dreamers, searchers, storytellers, writers, listeners, singers ... people who come to explore or to rest on their spiritual/human journeys have found peace, adventure and new life during retreats at Bethany, located on the Georgian Bay shore of the Bruce Peninsula, Canada. Themed retreats from 3–7 days and 'breakaway days' have brought people of all ages together in community in the extended home of Ron and Rita Baker, who are Associates of the Iona Community.

Guests stay in the house or in neighbouring cottages. The 'Story Barn' is a place for session themes and other activities. The pebble beach is often a venue for morning 'awakening' or a late night campfire gathering and the garden becomes an outdoor room if the weather cooperates. The Bethany table is prepared with care and is a place for relaxed dining and conversation, where children are welcome.

During the past two years Bethany has been used less for themed retreats and more for guests looking for a much needed leisure break in busy lives. Storytelling is a regular feature. Occasional retreats are held as need arises and the Spirit calls.

~ From Ron and Rita Baker, Bethany, Millar Lake, Ontario, Canada

Grace from Stillicidia

Generous God,
we thank you for the riches of your bounty,
for fruits of the earth that sustain us.
As we share food and fellowship with each other,
renew our determination to work for justice in your world
so that the gifts you freely give
may no longer be hoarded by the few
but shared by all people.
Amen

~Helen Boothroyd

Helen Boothroyd and her husband Richard Moriarty run Stillicidia, a small Christian house of welcome in Northern England. Residential and day guests are offered the possibility of using the creative media of art and crafts to explore spirituality and prayer. A grace is always said before meals, focusing on God's gifts and the blessing of fellowship, to help us to look beyond ourselves to the Gospel imperative of global justice.

Readings:

Psalm 133
John 13:6–17
Acts 2:1–21
1 Corinthians 12:4–13
Colossians 3:12–17
1 Thessalonians 5:11–28
Hebrews 12:1–2

Silent
GRACES

A Quaker grace

There is a story about a Quaker child who was invited to a meal at the house of an Anglican friend of his. The family said grace before the meal and the Quaker child said with interest, 'In our family we just sit quietly and smell our food.'

~ From Beth Allen, General Secretary, Quaker Communications

In silence, without rite or symbol, we have known the Spirit of Christ so convincingly present in our quiet meetings that his grace dispels our faith-lessness, our unwillingness, our fears, and sets our hearts aflame with the joy of adoration. We have thus felt the power of the Spirit renewing and recreating our love and friendship for all our fellows. This is our Eucharist and our Communion.

~ From the Quaker Yearly Meeting, 1928

A Corrymeela Community grace

In Northern Ireland religious words are 'loaded' and sometimes even dangerous. At the very least, they can mark out who belongs to us and who to them. It is not just words. Forms of prayer and ways of praying can be identified with either the Catholic or Protestant tradition.

So, Corrymeela decided to adopt a Quaker tradition of using silent grace for meals while asking people to give thanks for the food in their own way. In the silence we encourage people to think of those who provide the food and prepare our meals, to give thanks to the Creator for providing for our needs.

In this way, we hope people may express their thanks without the distraction of sectarian thoughts.

~ Trevor Williams, Leader of the Corrymeela Community

Corrymeela is an ecumenical Christian community committed to reconciliation in Northern Ireland. There are two hundred members, Catholics and Protestants. Corrymeela's residential centre seeks to be a safe space where people can meet across Northern Ireland's social, political and religious divides and share their stories. Corrymeela Knocklayd is a retreat centre exploring ecumenical spirituality. Corrymeela Reading resources Corrymeela Support Groups in England and Wales.

Pinderbat – the monks received in silence

The Buddhist monks at Piboon, near the Laos border in Thailand, depend on 'Pinderbat' for their one and only meal of the day, which is taken around 8:30 am in silence. During my stay at their island monastery I joined them one morning for their daily Pinderbat which means almsround.

I rose at 4:15 am. The monks were already chanting in the sala, their communal praying and eating place, in which a larger-than-life Buddha takes dominant position. As we arrived at the boathouse, the rocks and lake took on colour and a new day began. Five saffron-dressed monks and I left in the long boat; the sky was clear, clouds in the distance so colourful as the sun rose. We motored over the lake and three monks disembarked; walking barefoot, each had an umbrella and a begging bowl. We walked through dusty, red country lanes past the occasional wooden house on stilts, the senior monk leading the silent line, everyone three paces apart with me at the rear, head shaven and in white baggy clothes. As we approached houses, people – mainly women – would come to the roadside, kneel, and raise their offering to their forehead. The donor then placed a little of what they had in each monk's bowl. Nearly everybody gave sticky rice, the staple diet. Also donated were bananas and other fruits, eggs, but mainly sticky rice. (So much food that each day back at the sala a large enamel bowl of it was sent to the kitchen before the monks started to eat.) It began to drizzle halfway round, but we just put up our umbrellas; people came out in the rain. Most homes ignored the monks, one in eight giving a token something. The wealthier-looking places gave nothing.

By 7 am we had arrived further around the lake where two other monks waited with the boat. The monks received in silence – no acknowledgement; the belief is that the donor is the receiver by getting merit for the next life.

~ *Alan Hawkins*

Some quotes from Taizé

… The silence sometimes observed during a meal offers refreshment when you are tired, or communion in prayer for the companion who is sharing bread with you.

~ *Brother Roger, Taizé*

At table, times of silence bring peace of heart.

~ *Brother Roger, Taizé*

Readings:

1 Kings 19:12–14
Psalm 37:7
Psalm 46:10
Mark 4:39
Luke 1:20
Luke 4:1–3
Luke 23:9

One body in
YOUR NAME

Bread for all

May there be bread for all,
may the broken be made whole,
may we become one body in your name.

~ Jan Sutch Pickard

Pilgrim hope

O Spirit, we love you;
renew our pilgrim hope.
And may we, though many,
become one,
deep in the heart of God.

Amen, shalom, amen

~ *Words and music:* da Noust

A CTBI grace

Living God:
in Christ's death you expose the lie of our division
and in Christ's risen life you unite us again in freedom.
As we gather round this table
we thank you for the food we are about to share.

May it help keep us faithful to our calling as Churches working together
that we may glorify your name in the world
and embody your love for the people of our four nations.
Through Jesus Christ our Lord.
Amen

Churches Together in Britain and Ireland was set up by the churches in the four nations of these islands so that they could think, pray and work together. CTBI co-ordinates the work of the churches particularly in the areas of living spirituality, international affairs, church life, inter-faith relations, mission, international students, black Christian concerns, racial justice, church and society. (CTBI)

We praise and bless you

Eternal God, we praise and bless you for the constant
goodness you show us. Be with us at this meal as we
celebrate your gifts and our oneness.

~ Stella Durand

A Malagasy saying

'Those who are one in food are one in life.'

~ Source unknown

Oneness with your world

As we share this food, O loving God,
increase our oneness with your world
and with each other,
in the name of Christ.
Amen

~ *Maureen Edwards*

The holy things of God

The holy things of God are here,
blest and broken, quenching fear;
God's holy people, gather near,
made one with the tears of love.

If we but knew the gift he brings,
how he longs to gather in,
and share with us the living spring
cascading to our hearts.

In Christ there is no east or west,
one the host, and one the guests
whom Jesus kneads with holiness;
made one in the heart and love.

~ da *Noust*
  Tune: *Taladh Chriosda, Gaelic traditional*

In the heart of God

In the heart of God, only goodness,
in a human heart, cry of longing;
when our lives are joined together,
see a new world come, come to birth there –
in a covenant with the joiner's son.
God the Spirit comes, we are made one;
when our lives are joined together
see a new world born – alleluia!

~ da *Noust*
  Tune: *Exaltabo Te, Taizé*

A sign of your peace

Blessed are you, Lord God of Creation,
giver of all that is good.
God of peace, God of justice,
bless us and this bread we share,
that we may be one in heart and mind,
a sign of your peace on earth.
Just as the bread which we break,
once scattered as grain upon the hills,
has been gathered and made one,
so gather your children together and make us one.
For yours is the kingdom, the power and the glory,
now and for ever.

~ *CAFOD*

Spirit of Justice, Way of Love

Spirit of Justice, Way of Love,
    forever absent, forever full.
We come to this table in the midst of your people
    to partake of your presence
    through the fruits of the earth;
to share your power by the work of our hands;
    to reap your harvest everlasting in the human heart.
Fill our emptiness where we hunger,
    empty our surfeit where we overflow.
By your grace, let us be servants of one another,
    bringers of peace to all the earth,
and bearers of joy and love to all earth's children.
    Amen

An Abraxan invocation for a universal Eucharist, to be spoken in alternation, by a congregation divided right and left. However, it could also be the blessing for any special meal.

~ From Richard Boeke, Congregation of Abraxas, Unitarian Church

Food for our souls

God the Creator, thou hast made the bread.
Christ the Redeemer, thou hast changed it.
Holy Spirit, the Binder, thou dost convey it:
bread for our touching, food for our souls:
even as lives are bound together in thee.

~ George MacLeod

Community and communion

This is community, this is communion:
to eat together and give thanks.
Amen

~ *Ian M. Fraser*

Readings:

John 17:20–26
Acts 17:22–34
1 Corinthians 8:1–9
1 Corinthians 12:26–27
Galatians 3:28–29
Ephesians 4:1–16
Colossians 3:1–17

Body &
SOUL

Christ came in a body

'The gospel claims the key to all material issues is to be found in the mystery that Christ came in a body: and healed bodies and fed bodies: and that he died bodily and himself rose in his body, to save man body and soul.'

~ George MacLeod

Grace

Thank you, our God, for giving us so many things richly
to enjoy; and for the health and strength to enjoy them.

~ Stella Durand

Ethiopian grace

Bless this meal;
let it be for those
who receive it
healing
for the soul
and strength
for the body.

Amen

(In some parts of Ethiopia it is believed that you bring an angel with you to the dinner table.)

~ *Adapted from the liturgy of the Ethiopian Orthodox Church/Christian Aid*

May we laugh together

As we eat together
may we laugh together,
and know God's blessing
body and soul.

~ *Chris Polhill*

Bless to us, O God

Bless to us, O God,
our souls that come from on high.
Bless to us, O God,
our bodies that are of earth.
Bless to us, O God,
each thing our eyes see.
Bless to us, O God,
each sound our ears hear.
Bless to us, O God,
each odour that goes to our nostrils.
Bless to us, O God,
each taste that goes to our lips,
each note that goes to our song,
each ray that guides our way.
Amen

~ *Celtic traditional,*
   from Angelika Monteux, Camphill Rudolf Steiner School, Aberdeen

Today, tomorrow, yesterday

reflectively

To - day, to - mor - row, yes- ter-day

Time is gi - ven for___ us to share.

Sus - tained by food___ ev -'ry day

It's our souls that need your lov - ing care.

To - day, to - mor - row, yes- ter - day

Time is gi - ven for___ us to share.

Sus-tained by food__ ev-'ry day

It's our souls that need your lov-ing care.

To-day, to-mor-row, yes-ter-day

Time is gi-ven for__ us to share.

Sus - tained by food___ ev -'ry day

It's our souls that need your lov - ing care.

~ Text & music: Pat Livingstone, Oran

Soul food

Lord God, let us not add to gratitude for nourishment of
our bodies a plea that our souls may be likewise nourished;
but recognise that nourishment of bodies also sustains souls.
Amen

~ Ian M. Fraser

Grace

Dear God, grant us sustenance for body, mind and spirit, and compassion
for those less fortunate than ourselves.
Amen

~ *Jenni Sophia Fuchs*

Graces for those with digestive disorders

God be in my eating,
bless to my body this food for my healing.
The Creator of each cell bless me;
the Son, who ate with friends,
bless my digesting;
all-knowing Spirit bless my absorbing.
The Three in One weaving light in my gut
bless my expelling.
The One in Three nourish me
Body and Soul.
Sing praise to God who made me,
Creator, Son and Holy Spirit.

~ *Chris Polhill*

Praise be to God for food that is healing,
praise be to God for guts that are working,
praise be to God for this meal before us.

~ *Chris Polhill*

Loving God,
set your blessing on this food,
on this eating,
on the absorbing.
Set your blessing on this medicine,
with its healing,
with your healing.
And Alleluia anyway.

~ Chris Polhill

Grace for someone who is anorexic or bulimic

God, help me to keep this down.
Help me to love my body
and heal the pain that I find in eating.

~ Rosie Miles

Help me respond to my body's needs and hungers

Loving God,
help me respond to my body's needs and hungers,
help me to look after myself
free from guilt and fear
in the knowledge that I am worthy.
Amen

~ Claire Carson

As you see my body

Loving God,
at this meal
may I see my body as you see it,
may I will to eat as you would will it,
may your grace cover me.

~ Chris Polhill

Food for my body's needs

Loving Mother,
so nourish me from your breast,
that I may see food as it is.
Not as control,
not as filling the emptiness
you alone can satisfy,
but as food for my body's needs;
enough for each day.

~ Chris Polhill

Help me to know when I am hungry

Help me to know when I am hungry and when I am full.
Help me to know what I should do.
Help me not to deny myself
as some people have taught me to do.
Help me to accept what is rightfully mine.

~ Claire Carson

Sharing table fellowship

I've felt excluded for so long.
I long for the time when I can come around the table with others.

Help me to enjoy table fellowship again,
where I can offer hospitality
sharing food and myself with others.

~ *Claire Carson*

A Castle Craig grace

We thank thee Lord who daily, hour by hour,
gives us the blessings of the higher power
and in Thy bounteous generosity
the food we need for our recovery.
Help those who suffer still, O Lord, and then
all of us in Castle Craig.
Amen

~ *David Johnson*
Castle Craig is a drugs and alcohol recovery centre in Scotland

Gratitude – a remedy

I was made aware of the importance of gratitude in our life some years ago
when a good friend who was an instructor at a missionary school in the
State of New York asked me whether I had expressed thanks for the air I had
inhaled that day. In a way, this unexpected question startled me, because I
had never before thought of expressing gratitude for this indispensable gift,

but had for years taken for granted its being there to receive daily. Of course, I am sure that I am not alone in having been thoughtless in this respect. At the same time, I realised that I had reason to be grateful for many other precious gifts. Moreover, I became conscious of the fact that everyday life with its hectic demands and its various joys, but also its many obstacles, often crowded out the invaluable precious things we receive from the Giver of all good and perfect gifts at no cost to us whatsoever. Once we have begun to realise that, in spite of many difficulties, we have reason to be grateful for all the indispensable things that we cannot produce ourselves, then the awakening gratitude will permeate our being with a warm feeling, and this inner warmth is a gift of which we can always avail ourselves without cost.

Many years later I was living among the carefree inhabitants of a small South Sea island. I was curious about the cause of their happiness and found that they subscribed to gratitude without thinking. They never forgot to express gratitude for all the many little and greater joys the Creator gave them day by day. Without tiring they felt grateful for the sunshine, the warmth, the blue sea with its abundance of food, the coconut trees, various fruit trees and many other things. Gratitude not only transmits warmth, it also produces contentment, which in turn awakens happiness. It stimulates the endocrine glands, promotes good circulation, and thus influences the metabolism for better health, with all the important body functions being activated. The German poet Schiller once described joy as an animating spark, believing that joy in fact makes the world tick. With two world wars behind us, and all the subsequent wars, we realise that the spring in the world clock can be equally well wound by destructive powers. However, since these powers are never able to rob us entirely of the divine gifts of light, sunshine, air and others, we have reason enough to express our joy about them daily.

~ Dr H.C.A. Vogel

Readings:

Psalm 139:13–15
Isaiah 42:5
Mark 7:14–23
Luke 8:55
Luke 1:46–47
John 5:1–9
1 Thessalonians 5:23

All-humorous
MOTHER & FATHER

Cornflake grace

O Lord, grant that we may not be like cornflakes: lightweight, empty and cold; but like porridge – warm and comforting and full of natural goodness.

From Scottish Churches House [12]

Porridge

For porridge which runs on the spoon, we give thanks.
But for porridge which calls for knife and fork our praise is boundless.
Amen

~ Ian M. Fraser

Tallie's grace

At age 3, Taliesin's approach to the start of the day, leading to breakfast, is often as follows. The turnaround from line seven has something in common with the Psalms.

No morning!
No up!
No downstairs!
No breakfast!

No bix *(= his word for cornflakes)*
Breakfast?
Breakfast!
Hooray!
Amen!

~ Taliesin Coleman and David Coleman

The Chief Chef

presto!

Og - ling, gobb - ling, nosh - ing,

sipp - ing, slurp - ing, sa - vour - ing.

Thanks to God the Chief Chef.

~ Text & music: Pat Livingstone, Oran

We thank you Lord for the food we have

(This grace, sung to the tune of 'Twist and Shout', was used on Iona one Sunday lunch)

Leader:	We thank you Lord for the food we have
All:	(for our food)
Leader:	For peas and sprouts
All:	(peas and sprouts)
Leader:	We thank you Lord for the love you give
All:	(for your love)
Leader:	Help us to share it out
All:	(share it out)
Leader:	Oh, this food looks so good
All:	(looks so good)
Leader:	And it tastes so fine
All:	(tastes so fine)
Leader:	And it'll give us energy
All:	(en-er-gy)
Leader:	For praising God all the time
All:	(all the time)
All:	Ah. Ahh. Ahhh. MEN!

~ Jane Bentley

Grace for children

Leader:	Bread and pizza, tea and coffee,
All:	Eat and drink with thanks to God.
Leader:	Eggs and bacon, crisps and toffee,
All:	Eat and drink with thanks to God.
Leader:	Sunday lunch with roasted beef,
All:	Eat and drink with thanks to God.
Leader:	Sweets that stick all round your teeth,
All:	Eat and drink with thanks to God.
Leader:	Mother's milk for real beginners,
All:	Eat and drink with thanks to God.
Leader:	Do I dare suggest school dinners?
All:	Eat and drink with thanks to God.
Leader:	Jam that's sticky, toast that's crumby,
All:	Eat and drink with thanks to God.
Leader:	Everything that's scrummy yummy,
All:	Eat and drink with thanks to God.
Leader:	All this given for our pleasure,
All:	Eat and drink with thanks to God.
Leader:	God is good beyond good measure,
All:	Eat and drink with thanks to God.

~ Peter Graystone

Pizza grace

'Everyone can agree on pizza.'
 (Overheard in a restaurant)

God bless mushrooms
God bless green peppers
God bless olives
God bless onions
God bless pepperoni
God bless hot peppers
God bless double cheese
God bless _____
God bless the free and perfect art of the pizza makers
God bless the restless waiting
God bless the smell from the oven
God bless this beautiful, hot pizza we break and share.
Alleluia!

A different voice might be used for each topping

~ Neil Paynter

A Scottish grace

Pit doon yer heid, and up yer paws
an thank the Lord for good strong jaws

~ The Rt Rev. Patrick Rodger

A guest at Scottish Churches House called this grace 'The Glasgow grace'

Two graces sung to the tune of Frère Jacques

For this good food, for this good food,
for our friends, for our friends,
and this time together, and this time together,
thank you God, thank you God.

~ Morag Wilkinson

Deep-fried Mars bar, deep-fried Mars bar,
mushy peas, mushy peas,
bread and butter pudding, bread and butter pudding,
yum, yum, God! Yum, yum, God!

This grace may be adapted if the actual meal fits the tune

~ Morag Wilkinson

So much choice
A 3-part round. Children love this song!

Baked beans and bar-be-cue crisps,
chick-en cur-ry and fish and chips,
lem-on-ade and Chin-ese rice; we
thank you, God, for so much choice.

ostinato   (click fingers)

so   much   choice

~ Text & music: Pat Livingstone, Oran

Procrastination grace (two voices)

1. God we really just
    you know
    just really really
    really just
    just really want to
    oh so dearly really, nearly, sincerely

2. Get on with it
    and eat.
    Amen

~ David Coleman

For this grub

Thanks God for this grub,
thanks God for this spread,
and many thanks, so many thanks,
that we can gob it down now.

~ Chris Polhill

Twee grace

All-humorous father and mother of all
may we not be like twee graces
smug, sickly and sadly memorable

But in what we share here
may our grace be yours
surprising and feeding and building
the people you love
Amen

~ David Coleman

Mosquito grace

I thank you God that all day and night
there are always more people to bite.

~ Rosie Miles

Grace for cats

Bless the cat door that lets me in
Bless the hand that opens the tin.

~ Rosie Miles

Thank you God, Amen

moderato

Mar - ma - lade or jam or spread,

Pea - nut_ but - ter or___ crisp fresh bread,

Por - ridge, cer - eal, milk that may

Give_ us_ strength_ for God's work to - day.

Thank - you God, A - - men.

contd.

Note: This song has a number of verses for different meals. The idea is that you only have to learn one tune to provide graces for a whole day – useful for a short conference.

Breakfast: Marmalade or jam or spread,
peanut butter on crisp fresh bread.
Porridge, cereal, milk that may
give us strength for God's work today.
Thank you God, Amen.

Fried bread, bacon, sausage and eggs,
put energy in my tired legs.
Tomatoes, mushrooms and orange juice
stop me shaking like a wobbly mousse.
Thank you God, Amen.

Lunch: Half has gone, but half to come,
this day is halved by this mealtime song.
Thanks for food to speed our way
and energy enough for the rest of the day.
Thank you God, Amen.

Tea-time: Bread and cheese and jam on toast
and all the things we love the most.
Choc'late biscuits, coffee cake
we thank you God for all you make.
Thank you God, Amen.

Dinner: For all that's good, for all that's right
              we give You thanks for this meal tonight.
              The daily cycle of work and rest,
              hunger and food, You always give the best.
              Thank you God, Amen.

~ Text & music: Pat Livingstone, Oran

Readings:

Genesis 18:1–15
Genesis 21:6
Psalm 126:1–3
Psalm 149:1–5
Matthew 19:24
Luke 6:21
Acts 12:13–17

special
OCCASIONS

CHRISTMAS

Advent

God, the Father of mercies,
you willed your Son to take flesh,
in order to give life back to us.

Bless these your gifts
with which we are about to nourish our bodies,
so that, receiving new strength, we may wait in watchfulness
for the glorious coming of Christ.

~ From Dom Aidan Murray, OSB, The Worth Abbey Lay Community

All pilgrims need nourishment

Once they saw a star
that pointed to a promised land,
to a land of peace.
Peacemakers set out to follow that star.

It is both a joyful and arduous journey.
Sometimes a star shines brightly, the promise seems certain,
and the pilgrims can sing,
'How beautiful are the feet of those
who bring God's peace.'
Often the star disappears,
clouded over, hidden from view,

and the pilgrims grope blindly,
grow discouraged, get weary,
give thought to settling down,
to forgetting the promise of peace.

One thing is certain:
all pilgrims need nourishment
to sustain the journey.
An occasional oasis for the spirit
is essential,
a time to feast
on the refreshing waters,
the rich food of the spirit
in order to get strength
to continue the pilgrimage through darkness,
star-shine or not.

~ Mary Lou Kownacki, OSB/Pax Christi USA

Mary pounded grain

Oh Mary pounded grain, cooked and baked, fed the Christ child.
Through the work of others we too are fed.
We give thanks.
Amen

~ Ian M. Fraser

EASTER

Lent

We thank you, O Lord,
who gives us this food we eat.
We pray that you may also provide food
for those who are hungry
and gather all of us together at your heavenly kingdom.

We ask this through Christ our Lord.
Amen

~ *From Dom Aidan Murray, OSB, The Worth Abbey Lay Community*

Maranatha
(for two sets of voices)

I went down among the dead
sharing bread with all who long,
all who long to feed on me – maranatha
(x2)

When you leave the empty tomb
that your grieving heart has hewn,
you will long to call on me – maranatha
(x2)

When my Spirit comes on you,
all you do will be renewed,
you will long to be made free – maranatha

~ da *Noust. Music: Yezu Azal: Awo, Congolese Renewal* [13]

Lord, when you broke bread

Lord, when you broke bread with the two disciples at Emmaus you made scales fall from their eyes and they recognised you. Come to us now and enlighten the eyes of our mind to the reality of your risen presence and to the needs of others. Bless us and the bread we are about to break.
Amen

~ *Pax Christi*

A wedding anniversary grace

We thank you Father,
for patient, loving and forgiving spouses,
for lively and challenging children,
for loyal and trusted friends,
and for daily bread.
Be the honoured guest at this
_____ and _____'s
___th wedding anniversary celebrations.
Be their companion
in all their journeyings;
and the abiding source of joy
in all their pleasures.
So bless this food to our use
and ourselves in your service
for Christ's sake.
Amen

~ *Dick Acworth, Archdeacon of Wells*

It's your birthday

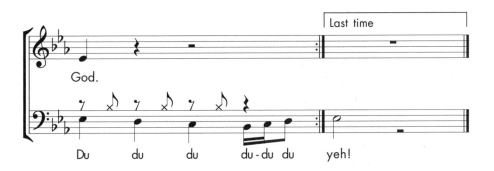

It's your birthday
let's celebrate
for life itself
so we resonate.
Thanks to God.

It's your birthday
let's celebrate
for all that's good
with this cup and plate.
Thanks to God.

It's your birthday
let's celebrate
the years you've lived
with this birthday cake.
Thanks to God.

~ Text & music: Pat Livingstone, Oran

Sung grace for anniversaries and birthday

Thank you Lord for giving us [name]
Thank you Lord for giving us [name]
Thank you Lord for giving us [name]
Right where we are.

Hallelujah praise the Lord
Hallelujah praise the Lord
Hallelujah praise the Lord
Right where we are.

~ From L'Arche Inverness, original source unknown

We've come to celebrate

Continue this pattern whilst singing.

We've come to ce - le - brate   Drink the__ drink and clear the plate.

Cantor: We've come to celebrate
All: We've come to celebrate
Cantor: Drink the drink and clear the plate
All: Drink the drink and clear the plate

Cantor:	We'd like to make a toast
All:	We'd like to make a toast
Cantor:	To this kind and generous host
All:	To this kind and generous host
Cantor:	Thanks for this mighty spread
All:	Thanks for this mighty spread
Cantor:	Those who cooked, prepared the bread
All:	Those who cooked, prepared the bread
Cantor:	This happy _____ (birthday/Christmas/Wedding) time
All:	This happy _____ time.
Cantor:	Dance and sing and drink the wine
All:	Dance and sing and drink the wine
Cantor:	This special _____ (Sabbath/Christening/evening) feast
All:	This special _____ feast
Cantor:	Have great fun, recall the least
All:	Have great fun, recall the least
Cantor:	Jesus your friends were wed
All:	Jesus your friends were wed
Cantor:	Wine from water when you said
All:	Wine from water when you said
Cantor:	A meal is a splendid thing
All:	A meal is a splendid thing
Cantor:	Thank you God, to you we sing
All:	Thank you God, to you we sing

~ *Text & music: Pat Livingstone, Oran*

NB Pick whichever verses are appropriate to your occasion. As the cantor sings a line that is repeated, no printed words or rehearsal are necessary ... and everyone can stamp their feet and clap.

Readings:

Song of Solomon 5:1
Isaiah 9:6–7
Mark 1:4–13
Mark 16:1–8
Luke 1:67–79
John 2:1–11
John 19:28–30

Each time
WE EAT

The wonder of your love

For the wonder of your love,
we give you thanks Lord.
Amen

~ *Ewan Aitken*

A grace in Kikongo

(spoken in parts of Congo and Angola)

E Nzambi, tutondele muna zola kwaku.
Tutondele muna madia mama.
Sambula mo: utusambula mpe.
Muna nkumbu a Mfumu eto Yisu Klisto. Amen

O God, we thank you for your love.
We thank you for this food.
Bless it, bless us also.
In the name of our Lord Jesus Christ.
Amen

~ *Provided by the late Ruth Page, a missionary teacher in Congo for many years
and in retirement a deacon at Bloomsbury Central Baptist Church.*

Each time we eat

Each time we eat, may we remember God's love.

~ *From China, source unknown*

Imela

Imela, imela, imela, Okaka.
Imela, Chineke. Imela Ony'oma.

Thank you, great God.
Thank you because you are good.

~ Traditional song from Nigeria

O taste and see

God, you have given us all kinds of plants,
those that bear grain and those that bear fruit.

O taste and see that the Lord is Good

You have given us your word and Law,
sweeter than honey.
Sweeter than honey dripping from the comb.

O taste and see that the Lord is Good

You have given us manna in the wilderness of our wandering
and daily bread to sustain.

O taste and see that the Lord is Good

For all you have given us,
generous, loving God
we praise you.

Amen

~ Neil Paynter

Keep us good

God bless the cook/s
God bless the food
God bless us
and keep us good.

~ Ruth Burgess

Heavenly Father, we thank you
(Tanzania)

Ba - ba A - san - te,   Ba - ba A - san - te,
Ba - ba Mbi - ngu - ni A - san - te.

Baba Asante, Baba Asante,
Baba Mbinguni Asante.
Heavenly Father, we thank you.

~ Taught by Mr Samson Lutabingwa, Bukoba Diocese (Lutheran Church in Tanzania).
  Source: unknown. Language: Swahili
  From Victoria Rudebark

Thank you Jesus, Amen
(South Africa)

Si - ya - bon - ga A - men, Si - ya - bon - ga A - men. Si - ya - bon - ga A - men._____ Si - ya - bon - ga A - men.

Siyabonga Amen.

Thank you Father. Amen.

~ Taught by Chris Hendricks, Kimberley, South Africa. Language: Zulu
  From Victoria Rudebark

Let the blessed bless

'Benedictus benedicat per Jesum Christum Dominum Nostrum'

'Let the blessed bless, through Jesus Christ our Lord'

~ Traditional Latin grace
  From Murdoch MacKenzie

Prayer from Aotearoa

In Aotearoa (New Zealand) those of us involved with the struggle for justice for Maori have been challenged about our use of their language. It is not a clearcut rule which is easily followed. Rather it is a matter of respectful consideration. So I use Maori place names and will not offer you a grace in Maori. What I give instead is a prayer which is based on the structure used by Pakeha to respect those aspects of life valued by Maori.

Creator God,
Here in Whanganui-a Tara,
where Tara's family found food from sea and land,
remembering later Maori arrivals who adapted and settled
we give thanks for your presence.

In this place where Maori supported the early British settlers
with food and shelter,
we, of this mechanised generation,
give you thanks that the land and the sea, the many ancestors
and our friends feed our spirits.

We thank you for this meal, which will feed our bodies.

~ Catriona Budge

A simple grace in Croatian

Hvala ti, Gospode, za ovu hranu.

Thank you, Lord, for this food.

Dreamtime gone

Great for a quiet morning!

~ *Text & music: Pat Livingstone, Oran*

You turned on the day

Lord God, you turned on the day, we rose from sleep, there was food on the table. We give thanks for the day, for our awakening to it, for food. Amen

~ *Ian M. Fraser*

On a frosty winter morning

For thick,
three-fruit marmalade
on buttered toast
by a log fire
on a frosty winter morning
I am truly thankful.

~ Peter Millar

Breakfast

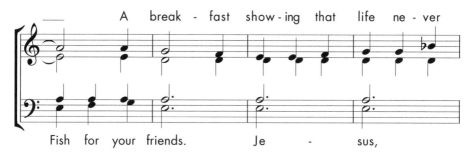

Each Time We Eat

~ *Text & music: Pat Livingstone, Oran*

Before you finish your breakfast

Before you finish your breakfast this morning, you've depended on half the world. This is the way our universe is structured.

~ Martin Luther King

Table grace for the middle of the day

God, we pause in the middle of the day
to gather our thoughts.
Our thoughts go out to you.

When we become hungry
half way through the day,
you are there
to strengthen us.

When we grow weary in the middle of the day,
you are there
to refresh us
and to help us move forward.

We lift up those
who are precious to us.
Be with them.
Be with all, too, who live with unmet needs.

Silent prayer

Bless our table fellowship

and give us grateful hearts
for all that you bestow upon us.
Amen.

~ Fritz Baltruweit, English translation by Jeffrey Myers

This grace has been used many times at the biennial assemblies of the German Protestant 'Kirchentag'.

Fridge grace

Lord, in the midst
of all my rushing around
can I open the fridge
and thank you
for all the goodies in it.

~ Peter Millar

Grace for a snack

For food that nourishes and
prayer that refreshes

in this fast and busy world,

Thanks, God.

~ Neil Paynter

A grace for a Devon cream tea

God bless these scones with the lightness of Devon air
God bless this cream with the heaviness of Devon cows
God bless this jam with the sweetness of Devon fields
and as we eat, God strengthen us to climb these narrow Devon lanes

~ Nicola Slee

Aeroplane meal blessing

God bless flight attendants who serve so cheerfully.

God bless the traveller in the seat beside me
    (God bless our small talk
    and the little space
    we share).

God bless my fellow passengers –
a great cloud of witnesses –
bumping and soaring through the heavens
surrounded by all the saints and angels.

God bless this meal.
May it contain more nourishment and energy than the in-flight movie.
May it help to get us through the long haul, the wait at customs,
the fight at baggage claim.
Amen

~ Neil Paynter

Prayer for an aeroplane meal

God, help me to take real time to remember
the hungry people in the countries which I am flying over;
the good earth below.

God forgive the mountain of paper and plastic on my dinner tray.
Help me to live in a more grounded, committed way.
Amen

~ Neil Paynter

The writing on the wall

GOOD FOOD IS A JOY
BE HAPPY FROM THE INSIDE OUT
SHARE YOUR TIME, THOUGHTS AND FOOD

~ Painted on the café wall of a motorway service station, source unknown

Campsite grace

Thank you God
that there is nothing quite like cooking food under a wide open sky.

Bless this simple, warming meal to us now,
and bless our single-ring gas burner
for it shall enter the kingdom of heaven.

~ Rosie Miles

Our holy convocations

high teas
takeaways

barbecues
banquets

brunches
lunches
wedding feasts

buffets
fry-ups

potlucks
picnics

breakfasts on the road
candlelit dinners
fish suppers.

God bless our holy convocations
Jesus, be our guest
Amen

~ Neil Paynter

Grace for a fast

In my hunger
I listen for your voice
I am empty before you
                    waiting

~ Rosie Miles

A grace for distracted eaters

Today my food has no flavour.
I do not notice what the weather is doing.
I eat distractedly, consumed by my own absorptions.
Still I make this prayer and my lips utter
Thanks.

~ Nicola Slee

Food and stomachs

What an imagination you have, Lord God.
Dreaming up food and stomachs.
Matching them.
Brilliant!
Amen

~ Ian M. Fraser

We are what we eat

Loving Creator,

We are what we eat

We become what we already are –
atoms of carbon, hydrogen, oxygen and nitrogen (for starters!)

Our food – created dust – reassembled again and again by living DNA.

What wonders!

Thank you, Loving Designer, for proteins, carbohydrates, and even fats,
to nourish and sustain us.

Please use our energies for your Kingdom.

Amen

~ David Hawkey

Out of the universe

Out of the universe, this star. Out of the star, this company – fed!
We marvel and give thanks.
Amen

~ Ian M. Fraser

A grace after sickness

After vomiting, I rise and eat again.
The food that I could not stomach yesterday
tastes of earth and heaven.
I chew bread slowly.
I sip water.
I marvel that I am upright.
It is enough.

~ *Nicola Slee*

Grace for lovers

No one tastes like you
and you are such a feast for my senses
I am body full to bursting with thankyous.

~ *Rosie Miles*

Breastfeeding grace

For the baby who sucks at my breast
and takes her life from me:
may she always be nourished and cherished
and may she grow strong and gentle and whole.

~ *Rosie Miles*

Youth grace

Dear God, though we may be young and healthy, and lack neither food nor drink, let us not forget the weak and the poor, those who hunger and those who thirst, as we give thanks for this meal.
Amen

~ Jenni Sophia Fuchs

A POEM AND A GRACE

How come?

If there are mountains of butter and lakes of wine,
then how come babies starve?
And if one man can be paid in millions,
then how come so many must live on the streets?
And if all men are brothers, my friend,
then how come we're at war?

If all are equal under the law,
then how come the prisons are full of the poor?
And if religion preaches a message of love,
then how come they can't agree?
And if all men are brothers, my friend,
then how come we're at war?

There is One who'll give food to the starving,
there is One who'll give homes to us all,

there is One who will free every prisoner,
he's the One who has shown us true love.

He'll settle all contradictions,
He'll make everything the way it should be,
and He'll change His world to what He had planned –
a fellowship of peace.

~ Morag Wilkinson

Grace for youth

God, on the TV news we see people starving,
people with nowhere to go.

When will we wake up, God?
When will we realise there is enough food for all, enough room for all?
When will we open our hearts and learn to share with our sisters
    and brothers?

It makes us feel angry, God.
And guilty, too.

God, help us to use our energies constructively.

Help us to use our passion and commitment
to work for change and to build a more generous, equitable world;
so that maybe by the time we are old we may see
the coming of your kingdom,
where all are fed and loved and set free.

God, thank you for this beautiful meal.

And for beautiful friends
who share our concerns and dreams and plans for action.

Amen

~ *Neil Paynter*

Two graces for students

Dear God, we give thanks for macaroni cheese and beans on toast, and we
are grateful for mum's home cooking to look forward to.
Amen

Dear God, as we give thanks for this meal, we ask that we may always have
sufficient food at the end of the month, plenty of chocolate to help us
through exams, and enough fry-ups to cure hangovers.
Amen

~ *Jenni Sophia Fuchs*

For smell, colour, taste

For smell, colour, taste ...
Thank you, generous,
amazing God.

May our lives be
a continual offering.
Amen

~ *Neil Paynter*

Yeast, salt and bread

Loving Creator of our food
we offer ourselves to you
as yeast to lighten your world from within
as salt to bring out your flavours of resurrection and hope
as bread to be blessed, broken and shared.
Amen

~ *David Hawkey*

Life in its fullness

God, help us to choose life in all its fullness
over substitutes that leave us sick and tired,
empty and wanting.

God bless this meal.
Amen

~ *Neil Paynter*

TEASPOON, FORK, KNIFE AND MUG PRAYERS

Reflections on using a teaspoon

As I measure out the salt to make the bread dough, I think of those who will eat it and share it; I remember those who are without bread this day; I ask you Lord, the bread of life, to fill and sustain me this day with your presence so that my life may glorify you.

~ From Traidcraft at Iona: Justice & Peace Prayers

Prayer on picking up a teaspoon

Lord, stir me today.
Mix in my fear with my confidence
my doubt with my faith
my strength with my weakness
and make me whole
like this cup of (fairly traded) tea.

~ From Traidcraft at Iona

Stir

Lord, stir my heart, stir my soul
and feed me with the food of the spirit.

~ From Traidcraft at Iona

Prayer relating to a fork

Lord, thank you for food and for farmers who sow and reap; for the suppliers who buy and transport; for the retailers who sell.

Help me not to be greedy and to eat only what is sufficient for my needs and for my appetite. Help me to remember that 'I should live simply that others may simply live'.
Amen

~ From Traidcraft at Iona

Fork

Thank you Lord for strength to lift this fork and food to fill it.

~ From Traidcraft at Iona

Knife

Lord, with this knife you have given me the power to hurt or to be useful. Please help me to use this and all that you have given me to help and not to harm. Lord, this knife is useless without its cutting edge. Please help me to be sharp and keen to work for you.

~ From Traidcraft at Iona

Prayer when drinking tea/coffee

O Lord, I thank you for this mug which enables me to drink,
this mug which reminds me of the cup
that You blessed long ago in an upper room.
Please, Lord, help me to drink spiritually, not just physically.
Give me a thirst O Lord to know more of you.
Amen

~ From Traidcraft at Iona

Blessing for new mugs

God who is both host and guest:
in Jesus, you sat at table
with all kinds of folk
and shared food and drink,
and talk about the Kingdom of God.
As we accept this gift
of mugs, may they be put to good use.
Bless the warm drinks that they will hold over the years
and may hearts be warmed too.
Bless the hands that will hold them,
the words that will be spoken over them,
and the sharing that they represent
in Jesus' name. Amen

~ Jan Sutch Pickard

GOD'S GRACE

Give us grace

Lord,
without your gifts we cannot live.
Without your grace we cannot learn to give.
So give us food
and give us grace
that in the needy we may see your face.

~ Eddie Askew

Grace our table

Lord grace our table with your presence
grace our minds with your understanding
grace our footsteps with your guidance
and grace our hearts with your unending love.

Amen

~ Sheila E. Auld

Give us the grace to pause

We are ready to eat, O God.

But give us the grace to pause
just long enough to notice our hunger
and appreciate our meal.

Give us the grace to pause
and think of those who are not hungry
because they have lost their appetite for life.

Give us the grace to pause
and pray for those who are too hungry
because they have nothing to put on their plate.

Now let us eat,
but mindfully,
O God.

Amen

~ *Brian Woodcock*

For the gifts of every day

For the gifts of every day
and the grace to enjoy them

Thank you God.
We are so fortunate.

~ *Neil Paynter*

Pour your grace upon this table

Lord, pour your grace upon this table
that as we eat and drink
we may be aware that we are truly blessed
in the gifts of creation
in the warmth of friendship
and in the love of our Lord Jesus Christ.

Amen

~ *Sheila E. Auld*

Grace

For the grace of living
for the grace of savouring
for the grace of God
     in our lives
     at our table
     in our bodies
thanks be

~ *Nicola Slee*

November in Skara

Thousands of chestnuts

lying on the concrete slab
that paves the square

(Trees grow through neat spaces)

As I cross the street
I see many crushed and broken
                open
by the feet of townspeople

I fill my pockets with
a dozen, shiny chestnuts.

~ David Scott

Skara is a town in Sweden

The grace of humility

The grace of humility
  in the face of how we fail.
The grace of acceptance
  in the knowledge of Your Love.
The grace of gratitude
  for all that you provide.
The grace of commitment
  to work for justice in the world.
We ask for these gifts
From Your treasury of Love.

Amen

~ Yvonne Morland

Grace

The grace of our Lord Jesus Christ be beside us
the love of God be firmly inside us
the fellowship of the Holy Spirit spread out
among our families and friends
and may our joyful beginnings have even happier ends.

Amen

~ Sheila E. Auld

Readings:

Psalm 69:13
Luke 15:11–32
John 1:16–17
2 Corinthians 12:9
Ephesians 2:4–10
Hebrews 4:16
Hebrews 13:7–9

... and for
DESSERT

Oranges for dessert

When we've had oranges for dessert at L'Arche, we sometimes start chucking the peel about at the end of the meal. Everyone gets into it. An Englishman once asked me if this was a traditional French custom. I don't know about that! But I do know that it is one way to bring people out of their isolation to express themselves joyfully – especially if they can't communicate with words. People who cannot participate in interesting conversations can participate through play. When a piece of orange peel arrives on their nose, they are delighted – and they throw it back.

I was once explaining this way of celebrating during a retreat I was giving in New Zealand for superiors of religious orders. The last evening, we had a celebratory meal to which the bishop came. And, by chance, there were oranges for dessert. It was quite something to see those serious and until now rather formal mothers provincial joyfully chucking orange peel about under the astonished gaze of the bishop! He, of course, didn't know how it had all started. There was a bit of explaining to do!

~ Jean Vanier

Last summer's blueberries

Pipaluk lives in the Arctic where winter comes early
and summer comes late.

One day Pipaluk said to her mother,
The blueberries are ripe. Tommorrow I will pick them
and we will have them for supper.

But that night winter came early. Next morning
the land was covered with snow. Pipaluk put on

her kumiks and her parka and her fur mittens.
She looked for the blueberries. She looked and
looked and looked, but she could not find them.
They were hidden under the early winter snow.

Winter has come, said her father.
He brought the kayak up from the sea to
their house. Soon the sea was frozen and the sun
did not stay in the sky.

Pipaluk played in the white snow in the dark
winter days. She saw the Northern Lights
and she forgot about the blueberries that were
covered by the deep white snow.

The winter went on and on and on.

Then the sun began to stay longer in the sky.
One day Pipaluk's mother said,
Look, the snow is melting!
Pipaluk put on her boots and her warm parka
and her fur mittens and went outside.

The snow was going away. It was making little
rivers and running away towards the sea.
Every day Pipaluk saw the snow melting.

Her father mended the kayak.
Soon the ice will go out and we will catch fish, he said.
And soon Pipaluk saw patches of bare brown earth
on the hills. The snow was running away to the sea.
The land began to look green.

I will look for some flowers for you,
Pipaluk said to her mother.

She put on her boots and went out to play
in the running snow water.
She found some white flowers growing in the
fresh green moss;
and then she saw the berries. They were blue
and soft and ripe.

Pipaluk ran to tell her mother,
I have found the blueberries!
They were hidden under the snow all winter,
said her mother.
Pipaluk took a pail and went outside.

And that evening, Pipaluk and her mother and
her father all had last summer's blueberries
for supper.

~ Rita Baker

I have a friend who lived in Baker Lake, Northwest Territories, Canada for several years. She told me about children in the community picking frozen blueberries in the spring. I was touched by the story and wrote Last Summer's Blueberries.

Kiwi fruit

Cora asks for a kiwi, and I pass her the fruit basket. There's something beautiful and moving about an old woman eating a kiwi fruit, noisily. Everyone else is sitting around eating dry silence.

'So, how old are you now Cora?' I ask to make some conversation. 'Ninety-three?'

'Yes, I think so,' she says.

'I guess you must have seen a lot of changes.'

'Oh yes ... When I was nursing my second husband he looked up at me and asked, "Will it be long?" I didn't know what to say.'

'Did he ... live very long?'

'I really don't know. Things are getting vague, you know ... My first husband died and left me with four children.'

'That must have been hard.'

'Oh, if they told you before what you'd have to go through in life,' says Cora, 'you'd throw up your hands,' but laughs, kiwi juice trailing down her old veined hand, shining on her chin.

About a month later, Cora and I go to church together. During communion she closes her eyes and smiles, and the look on her face is the same as when she ate the kiwi fruit.

~ Neil Paynter, from a short story about working at a rest home for the elderly

Prayer

Christ, you are present in bread and in wine,
in kiwi fruit and in old women,
in all that gives us life.
May we be always open to recognising you.
Amen

~ Neil Paynter

A summer fruits grace

I will eat this cherry as if it were the first and last from the tree
I will savour this peach as if it were the only one
I will relish this mango as if it were the harvest of paradise
I will worship this fruit as if it were the body of God

~ Nicola Slee

Grapes

You need the grapes
to make the wine
the grapes that grow
together on the same stem
drawing the same life-giving sap
from the vine
tended by the same vine dresser
but growing together
touching
ripened by the same sun.
Together – in a bunch
shielding each other
protecting each other
supporting each other
yet each grape a complete unity
a whole fruit.
These are the grapes – that make
the wine – the joy –

the celebration
these grapes that grow
together.

~ *Ruth Burgess*

The fruit (salad) of the Spirit

It is the season of fruit salads. From my childhood in Nairobi, I have loved exotic fruit salads: papayas (paw-paws), mangoes, passion fruit, grapes, bananas and pineapples. Try this tasty and colourful mix yourself!

On my last visit to Kenya in August 2000, fruit and other foods were less abundant. Central and Southern Africa are now blighted by drought, putting 13 million lives at risk through food shortage and insecurity ...

Hunger, rooted in poverty, is the biggest destroyer of human life today. It is a form of terrorism. It is torture for parents helplessly to watch children die of hunger ...

Bob Geldof recently described African poverty as 'imposed poverty' which can be removed. He was supporting a Christian Aid challenge for the Prime Minister to 'listen' to African people. At the 2001 Labour Party Conference, Tony Blair said 'The state of Africa is a scar on the conscience of the world. But if the world as a community focused on it, we could heal it. And if we don't, it will become deeper and angrier.' It is part of our calling to challenge all forms of injustice. We can all do something to challenge western nations to promote fair trade rules ...

Eucharistic communities cannot be at ease while hunger terrorises people. Jesus Christ desires life in all its fullness for all. The fruit of the spirit is life.

~ *Inderjit Bhogal*

Fruits of the spirit

quite fast

Chorus

Plums, pears, grapes, Fruit so jui - cy, Ap - ri- cots,

me - lon and figs. Or - ange trees, po - me - gran - ates,

al - mond tree, cin - na - mon, figs.

(If no melodic instrument use percussion)

Verse

1.

Women

1. Such rich - ness, Love and peace.

Men

God's Spi - rit, Pa- tience and joy___

Such rich - ness, self - con - trol.

God's Spi - rit ri - pens with - in___ us.

2. Self - con - trol grows in us.

Faith - ful - ness, hu - mi - li - ty___

Gen - tle - ness is God's gift.

Kind and good, Fruits from our God.___

~ *Text & music: Pat Livingstone, Oran*

Reading:

Galatians 5:22

For the END
of meals

A celebratory grace

To be read section by section
by each of the company in turn round the table,
perhaps at the end of a meal.

For the shepherds and the sheep,
for the roast lamb
that warms the meat-eaters,
and the wool
that warms the vegetarians

For the cattle ranchers and their herds,
for the beef and pork and bacon

For the gamekeepers,
and for the venison and the pheasants

For those who harvest waters fresh and salty,
and for their fish

For the poultry keepers,
for the hens and eggs,
the chickens and the guinea fowl

Thanks to the Creator of all

For farmers and their crops,
the maize and barley, wheat and rice

For mowers of hay
and gatherers into bales

For vegetable growers
and their allotments,
for the carrots and onions,
peas and beans, broccoli and cabbage,
potatoes and courgettes

Thanks to the Creator of all

For growers of herbs,
basil and rosemary, mint and bay leaves,
sage and parsley

For spices from the east,
cinnamon and ginger,
curry and paprika, cloves and nutmeg –
and garlic if it is discreet

Thanks to the Creator of all

For the fruit growers and their orchards,
for plums and peaches,
oranges and lemons,
apples and pears,
apricots and raspberries,
and for the makers of jams
and their kilner jars

For beekeepers and their hives,
for bees and the pollen and the honey

For olive tenders and their groves,

for olives green and black,
and for olive oil

And blessed be the cheesemakers
and the butter churners

Thanks to the Creator of all

For the hop-pickers and their beer

For the keepers of vineyards and their wines
and their dark mysterious cellars

For the distillers and their single malts

For juicers and for Vitamin C

For growers of coffee and tea,
for the pickers and the roasters

Thanks to the Creator of all

For sun and rain, soil and compost,
without which none of this at all

Thanks to the Creator of all

For flower growers
and their glasshouses,
the florists and the flower arrangers

For chandlers and their candles

For potters and their vessels,
the glaziers and their glasses

For spinners and weavers
and their cloths

For metal workers and their cutlery

Thanks to the Creator of all

For the bakers of loaves,
for the mysterious yeast,
for sandwiches and croissants

For oats and flakes and bran,
for nuts and sultanas,
for muesli and porridge

For bakers of cakes and pies,
and for the pastry cooks,
for teacakes and birthday cakes,
for toast and jams and marmalade,
for biscuits and crackers,
chocolate and crisps,
ice cream, mousse, and fools –
all of course in moderation –
except for now and then …

Thanks to the Creator of all

Now is the time for anyone
to give thanks for anything missed out –

or for their particular favourites,
from black puddings to nouvelle cuisine

For every food and drink
that nourishes us and gives us delight

Thanks to the Creator of all

For the makers and drivers of tractors

For seed merchants and harvesters,
the pickers and packers,
the distributors and shopkeepers

For supermarkets and farmers' markets

For deep freezes and the cool pantries

Thanks to the Creator of all

For the flair of cooks,
for their soups and salads,
sauces and secret ingredients

For those who can stand
the heat of the kitchen,
for those who lay tables
and those who clear away –
and for the patience of those
who wait upon us

Thanks to the Creator of all

For reunions and romance,
for celebrations and parties,
for fasting and feasting,
for families and friends,
for daily bread and heavenly banquet,
for hosts and guests
at one round table

THANK YOU! ALLELUIA! YES!

(All breathe out a long sigh of contentment)

~ Jim Cotter

The meal enjoyed

Thank you Lord for the lovely meal we have enjoyed and
for all your goodness to us.

~ Stella Durand

Lord, how glad we are

Lord, how glad we are that we don't hold you,
but that you hold us.

~ Author unknown, Haiti/CAFOD

Rune of the peat fire

The Sacred Three
to save,
to shield,
to surround
the hearth,
the house,
the household,
this eve,
this night;
oh, this eve,
this night,
and every night,
each single night.

~ Celtic traditional

To trust in grace

God, help us to live fully and openly and hopefully,
to trust in grace and
believe in resurrection.
Amen

~ Neil Paynter

Prayer

O most merciful Redeemer, Friend, Brother
may we know thee more clearly,
love thee more dearly,
follow thee more nearly
for ever and ever.
Amen

~ St Richard of Chichester

Alone with none but thee

Alone with none but thee, my God
I journey on my way.
What need I fear when thou art near,
O King of night and day?
More safe am I within thy hand
than if a host did round me stand.

~ Attributed to St Columba

Go forward

Go forward in God's strength.

~ Quaker Faith and Practice 29.10

As you have been fed

As you have been fed at this table
go to feed the hungry.
As you have been set free
go to set free the imprisoned.
As you have received – give.
As you have heard – proclaim.
And the blessing which you have received
from Creator, Son and Spirit
go with you.

~ Kate McIlhagga

God of the hungry

God of the hungry, the homeless, the helpless,
make us hunger and thirst till their rights prevail.
God of the stateless, the uprooted, the refugee,
make us hunger and thirst till their rights prevail.
God of the prisoner, the prophet, the protester,
make us hunger and thirst till your Word,
through them, is heard.
Amen

~ Jean Mortimer

Make us worthy

Make us worthy, O Lord, to serve
the men and women throughout the world
who live and die in poverty and hunger.
Give them, through our hands,
this day their daily bread,
and by our understanding and love,
give peace and joy.
Amen

~ *Mother Teresa*

Blessing

God bless each of us as we travel on.
In times of need
may we find a table spread in the wilderness
and companions on the road.

~ *Jan Sutch Pickard*

May we recognise you

O Christ, may we recognise you:

in companions gathered round the table and
in colleagues meeting around the water cooler

in mysterious strangers and
in transparent family members

in next door neighbours and
in brothers and sisters across the world

in everyone we meet, O Christ
and in all the places we share
our broken and beautiful lives.[14]

~ Neil Paynter

International peace prayer

O God,
Lead us from death to life, from falsehood to truth.
Lead us from despair to hope, from fear to trust.
Lead us from hate to love, from war to peace.
Let peace fill our hearts, our world, our universe ...
Amen

~ Based on an ancient Sanskrit invocation

Pledge of assistance

Isaiah 58:7–8

I pledge assistance
to the people
who suffer from hunger and violence
and to a new order
in which all stand
one family
interdependent
with liberty and justice
for all.

~ *George Amoss Jr, Bread Not Bombs*

It is not true

Voice: It is not true that we must accept
inhumanity and discrimination,
hunger and poverty,
death and destruction;

ALL: This is true:
I have come that they may have life,
and have it abundantly.

~ *From an affirmation from South Africa*

Prayer

O God, you promise a world
where those who now weep shall laugh;
those who are hungry shall feast;
those who are poor now,
and excluded,
shall have your kingdom of their own.
I want this world too.
I renounce despair.
I will act for change.
I choose to be included
in your great feast of life.
Amen

~ *Christian Aid*

One world – two tables

In Yoker St Matthews from time to time the congregation manage to get the minister out of the way and 'do' the Sunday morning service by themselves. On the Sunday of 'One World Week', the centre of the morning act of worship was not a wordy sermon, but a sitting down at two tables, a rich table and a poor table. I'm sure many church folk have shared this experiment at some time or another; there's no claim of originality in this.

As the congregation arrived for the morning service they were handed a ticket at random. As they came into the church they found that instead of being able to take their normal seats, they were placed round two tables, one small table with about a dozen seats and another great long, long table with umpteen seats. The small table was laden with goodies, dainty sausage rolls, sandwiches, cakes, chocolate biscuits, best china teacups, cutlery, sparkingly clean white table cloth, the best chairs taken out of the chancel and so on ... Oh, and a very posh candelabra, resplendent with candles. The long table on the other hand had no table cloth, no cutlery, stacking chairs, plastic cups, jugs of water and dry rolls.

The dozen or so 'lucky' folk with the tickets for the rich table sat down to their feast of goodies; the others, the 'unlucky' ones, were left with their bread and rolls.

Now, it was only a symbolic sort of thing and we shouldn't read too much into it, but a couple of things happened which I couldn't help but notice. The first was that those at the rich table just picked at their goodies and left the plates still brimming with sandwiches, cakes and biscuits. It may have been they didn't want to spoil their appetite before going home for their Sunday dinner, but it might have been more than that ... certainly, afterwards, some of them said they felt guilty or uncomfortable being at that table. At the poor table, every last bit of dry roll was scoffed up. Secondly, the rich table was a very quiet table, whereas the poor table was a hilarious riot ... coincidence, perhaps, perhaps not! One way or another the folk at the rich table did seem to be suffocating.

~ Erik Cramb

I believe

I believe, Lord, that
everything good in the world
comes from you.
I believe in your great love
for all people.
I believe that, because you
preached love, freedom and
justice, you were humiliated
tortured and killed.

I believe that you continue
to suffer in our people
risen in rebellion;
that you are present
in the far off wind
that carries the weeping
of the people
the oppressed who seek
their imprisoned freedom.
I believe there is no other
road, no other truth.
There is but one.
I believe that you call me
to defend your cause;

But I also believe
that you accompany me
in the task of transforming
this world
into a different one where
there is no suffering
or weeping;
A world where there is
a gigantic table
set with free food
where everyone is welcome.

I believe that you
accompany us in waiting for
the dawning of a new day,
I believe that you
will give us strength
so that death
does not find us without
having done enough,
and that you will rise
in those who have died
seeking a different world.

~ Anonymous, El Salvador/CAFOD

The king and the peasant

God decided to become visible to a king and a peasant and sent an angel to inform them of the blessed event.

'O King,' the angel announced. 'God has deigned to be revealed to you in whatever manner you wish. In what form do you want God to appear?'

Seated on his throne and surrounded by awe-struck subjects, the king proclaimed, 'How else would I wish to see God, save in Majesty and Power? Show God to us in the full glory of Power.'

God granted his wish and appeared as a bolt of lightning that instantly pulverised the King and his court. Nothing, not even a cinder, remained.

The angel then manifested herself to a peasant saying: 'God deigns to be revealed to you in whatever manner you desire. How do you wish to see God?'

Scratching his head and puzzling a long while, the peasant finally said, 'I am a poor man and not worthy to see God face to face. But if it is God's will to be revealed to me, let it be in those things with which I am familiar. Let me see God in the earth I plough, the water I drink, the food I eat. Let me see God in the faces of my family and neighbours.'

God granted the peasant his wish, and he lived a long and happy life. May God grant you the same!

~ Source unknown/Pax Christi USA

Creative absorption

'We are fed not by what we eat but by what we digest.'

Lord God, teach our stomachs the art of creative absorption of your good gifts. Amen

~ Ian M. Fraser

Haleluya! Pelo tsa rona

Christ the Lord to us said:
I am wine, I am bread
I am wine, I am bread
Give to all who thirst and hunger

Now he sends us all out
strong in faith free of doubt
strong in faith free of doubt
Tell all the joyful Gospel

~ From South Africa

Blessing

May you always stand tall as a tree,
be as strong as the rock Uluru,
as gentle and still as the morning mist,
hold the warmth of the campfire in your heart,
and may the Creator Spirit always walk with you.

~ Betty Pike

Uluru is the name used by the traditional custodians of the land for what was formerly known as Ayers Rock

Come the Day

Two groups of singers can alternate on each line

~ *Text: Amos 8: 11. Music: da Noust*

Readings:

Psalm 148
Proverbs 30:7–9
Isaiah 35:1–10
John 10:10–11
John 21:15–17
Romans 8:38–39
Revelation 21:5–7

Washing up

God is in every place, at the kitchen sink and at the table.

~ Quaker Faith and Practice 2.84

If the only prayer you ever said was 'Thank you',
you would have said all the prayers.

~ Meister Eckhart, medieval mystic

SOURCES AND ACKNOWLEDGEMENTS

Every effort has been made to trace copyright holders of all items reproduced in this book. We would be glad to hear from anyone whom we have been unable to contact so that any omissions can be rectified in future editions.

FRONT PAGE
George MacLeod, *The Coracle: Rebuilding the Common Life*, Foundation Documents of the Iona Community, May 1939

Washing one's hands – from *Prayers, Poems, Songs and Reflections from Latin America and the Caribbean*, compiled 2002, Christian Aid.

FOR THE HANDS (P13)

P14

From the hand of God – from *Meaning the Lord's Prayer*, The Very Rev. Dr George Reid, Wild Goose Publications (out of print).

A flame of love – Gaelic traditional prayer, from *The Iona Abbey Worship Book*, Wild Goose Publications, 2001, ISBN 1 901557 50 2.

P15

A prayer in Zulu – from *Graces from Around the World,* compiled by Richard Bowers, illustrated by Mark Westbrook, Bloomsbury Central Baptist Church, first published 1998; second edition 2001. Booklet sold in aid of the Development Fund of Bloomsbury Central Baptist Church. May be obtained by writing to Richard Bowers at Bloomsbury Central Baptist Church, 235 Shaftesbury Avenue, London WC2H 8EP. It sells for £2.00.
  Bloomsbury's 'Sunday Lunch' is legendary. Visitors from abroad mingle with Londoners, while homeless men and women enjoy the opportunity for a rest and a meal. Part of the legend is the 'grace' offered by Richard Bowers at one o'clock on the dot! *(Barrie Hibbert, Introduction to* Graces from Around the World*)*

You have poured your gifts – by Stella Durand, from *Graces: A Collection of Table Graces for Use Before and After Meals*, compiled by Stella Durand, home-produced and sold in aid of the Community of Aidan and Hilda.

P16

All things come from you – by Stella Durand, from *Graces: A Collection of Table Graces for Use Before and After Meals* (see note for p15).

P22

Thank you – by Richard Bowers, from *Graces from Around the World*, compiled by Richard Bowers (see note for p15).

P23

Linked together – extract from Wild Goose Issues 3, *Compassion in the Marketplace*, by Joy Mead, Wild Goose Publications, 1997, 0 947988 88 2.

P25

People far away © Christian Aid from the pamphlet *Time for Tea: Ideas for Use with Children at Harvest*. Christian Aid works in over 60 countries helping people, regardless of religion or race, to improve their own lives and to tackle the causes of poverty and injustice. *(Christian Aid)*

P26

Praise be to you – Syrian, 4th century, translated from *Evangelisches Gesangbuch*, 1st edition, Spener Verlagsbuchhandlung, Frankfurt/M, 1994. English translation by Jeffrey Myers.

OUR DAILY BREAD

P32

Sharing our bread – extract from the sermon 'Sharing Our Bread', in *Walking in Darkness and Light: Sermons and Reflections*, by Kathy Galloway, Saint Andrew Press, 2001, ISBN 0 715207 69 5.

P33

Willing sharers – by Stella Durand, from *Graces: A Collection of Table Graces for Use Before and After Meals* (see note for p15).

P35

'Prayers of concern' – prayer from 'Day Time Liturgy A', *A Wee Worship Book: 4th*

Incarnation, Wild Goose Worship Group, Wild Goose Publications, ISBN 1 901557 19 7.

P38

Bread – by Ruth Burgess, from *On Ground Level*, Ruth Burgess, Wild Goose Publications (out of print).

P41

'Loving God, take our hands' © Christian Aid. Also included in *Seeds for the Morrow: Inspiring Thoughts from Many Sources*, collected by Dorothy Millar.

GETTING OUR TEETH INTO THINGS (P43)

P44

Getting one's teeth into things – from the reflection 'The Bread of Life', in *Daily Readings with George MacLeod*, edited by Ron Ferguson, Wild Goose Publications, ISBN 1 901557 44 8. Originally published in *We Shall Rebuild*, p116.

P45

For all God's people – from *Prayers, Poems, Songs and Reflections from Latin America and the Caribbean*, compiled 2002, Christian Aid.

Living on nothing – from *Out of the Shadows: A Collection of Poems from the Fourth World*, edited by Liz Prest, ATD Fourth World, 2000, ISBN 0 950851 45 1. *Out of the Shadows* is an anthology of poetry from a creative writing project involving professional writers with over a hundred individuals who live in poverty in the UK. ATD Fourth World is a human rights organisation taking a holistic approach to poverty eradication. It believes that only by working in partnership with families experiencing poverty and social exclusion can real and effective change come about in the lives of those most disadvantaged. ATD Fourth World commemorates 17 October, International Day for the Eradication of Poverty.

P48

'O God, you have made us creatures of this earth' © Christian Aid, taken from the pamphlet *They Shall be Satisfied, Ideas for Harvest Worship and Giving*.

P49

If the hunger of others – from *Prayers, Poems, Songs and Reflections from Latin*

America and the Caribbean, compiled 2002, Christian Aid.

P50

Bread and butter – from *Peacemaking Day By Day: Daily Readings*, Pax Christi USA, 1996, ISBN 1 872370 05 5. Pax Christi International is a non-profit, non-governmental Catholic peace movement working on a global scale on a wide variety of issues in the fields of human rights, security and disarmament, economic justice and ecology. *(Pax Christi)*

P51

'Bendice, Señor, nuestro pan' – music annotation and Spanish transcription, Federico Pagura © 2002 World Council of Churches, PO Box 2100, 1211 Geneva 2, Switzerland. Used by permission.

P52

Feed the hungry – extract from 'Hunger on Butler Street: The Butler Street Breakfast', Part 3, from *A Work of Hospitality: The Open Door Reader, 1982–2002*, Peter R. Gathje, editor, The Open Door Community, Atlanta, ISBN 0 971589 30 5.

P55

Gabi, Gabi – from *Freedom Is Coming: Songs of Protest and Praise from South Africa* for mixed choir, collected and edited by Anders Nyberg, Wild Goose Publications, ISBN 0 947988 49 1.

P56

May we live more simply – adapted from a traditional Russian prayer, from *Iona: Pilgrim Guide*, Peter Millar, Canterbury Press, 1997, ISBN 1 853111 66 X

The water of life © Christian Aid, from *Water for Life* harvest appeal materials.

P57

Beans and toast – extract from the article 'Discerning Sufficiency, An On-going Theological Task', by Ian M. Fraser, *Coracle*, Issue No. 3/3: Having Your Cake: Christians and Money.

The simplicity of food – from *No Greater Love: Sources of Taizé*, Brother Roger of Taizé (A), Geoffrey Chapman Mowbray, a Cassell imprint. Originally published as *Amour de tout amour*, © Ateliers et Presses de Taizé, 71250 Taizé Community, France, 1990, translation Ateliers et Presses de Taizé, 1991.

P60

To do your work – by Mark Westbrook, from *Graces from Around the World*, compiled by Richard Bowers (see note for p15).

P63

When I give food to the poor – from *Prayers, Poems, Songs and Reflections from Latin America and the Caribbean*, compiled 2002, Christian Aid.

P64

'Isten, God of our confessing' – adapted by Rev. Richard Boeke from a free translation by Rev. Josef Kaszoni of an ancient Hungarian hymn, from *A Garland of Graces*, a selection of table graces from the worship committee, the General Assembly of Unitarian and Free Christian Churches. Original text p. 21 in *Uni-worship*, £6 or $10 including postage from Richard Boeke, 16 St Mary's Gardens, Horsham RH12 1JP. Last three lines of the original Hungarian hymn read: 'One, the blessed God we cherish/ Body, Soul, Wisdom nourish/ Faith and Freedom ever Flourish.'

CHRIST OUR HOST, CHRIST OUR GUEST (P69)

P72

They had virtually nothing yet ... – extract from *Exile in Israel: A Personal Journey with the Palestinians*, by Dr Runa Mackay, Wild Goose Publications, 1995, ISBN 0 947988 75 0.

P73

Trim the cruisie's failing light (Rune of Barra) – words: Rune of Barra; translation: Murdoch MacLean; Music: Wild Goose Resource Group/Iona Community, from *Common Ground: A Song Book for All the Churches*, Saint Andrew Press, 1998, ISBN 0 715207 53 9.

P74

St Columba and hospitality – extract from *Chasing the Wild Goose: The Story of the Iona Community*, by Ron Ferguson, Wild Goose Publications, ISBN 1 901557 00 6.

Extract from Adomnán's *Life of Columba* in *Adomnán's Life of Columba*, A.O. and M.O. Anderson, OUP, 1961.

P78

'Dear God, we thank you for the the richness, gifts and contributions of different cultures' – from *This Is the Day*, Wild Goose Publications, 2002, ISBN 1 901557 63 4. This prayer evolved out of a litany of celebration written for a justice and peace service on the subject of racial justice, which took place in Iona Abbey. Different staff members of the Iona Community were invited to contribute their ideas and details – Dorothy Millar, Neil Paynter, Jan Sutch Pickard, Helen Lambie, Jane Bentley …

P80

Jesus's best friends – extract from *The Gospel Truth and a Worldly Lie*, from *A Work of Hospitality: The Open Door Reader, 1982–2002*, Peter R. Gathje, editor, The Open Door Community, Atlanta, ISBN 0 971589 30 5.

P84

In the kitchen – from *Vice Versa*, by Jan Sutch Pickard, Church in the Marketplace Publications, 1997, ISBN 1 889147 12 8.

P86

To share what we have – from *A Taste for Peace: Recipes and Reflections*, Pax Christi, 1996, ISBN 1 872370 30 6. Written, compiled and edited by: Peggy Attlee, Sr Joyce Blackwell, Anne Burke, Brid Coady Weekes, Cecily Fernbank, Valerie Flessati, Pat Gaffney, Ellen Teague, Kathy Wicks. Illustrations by Trudie Thompson.

P87

Lord of Joy, come be our guest – from *Svenska Psalmboken* (The Swedish Hymn Book), Verbum, 1986. Hymn © Mrs Vivienne Stern. English translation © 2003 Victoria Rudebark.

P88

Stay with us Lord – from *The Iona Abbey Worship Book*, Wild Goose Publications, 2001, ISBN 1 901557 50 2.

P89

Sun behind all suns – from the prayer 'The Glory in the Grey', by George MacLeod, *The Whole Earth Shall Cry Glory*, Wild Goose Publications, 1985, ISBN 0 950135 18 6.

FAMILY, FRIENDS, FELLOWSHIP (P91)

P93

Lord of Life – by Peter Millar, from *An Iona Prayer Book*, Peter Millar, Canterbury Press, 1998, ISBN 1 853112 05 4.

P94

Strong, sheltering God – prayer from the liturgy 'Home', by Kathy Galloway, *The Pattern of Our Days*, Wild Goose Publications, 1996, ISBN 0 947988 76 9.

A family prayer – from *Meaning the Lord's Prayer*, The Very Rev. Dr George Reid, Wild Goose Publications (out of print).

Lord, if this day – prayer from Mexico, from *With All God's People: The New Ecumenical Prayer Cycle*, WCC Geneva, 2nd revised edition, 1990, page 261.

P99

An African saying – from *An Iona Prayer Book*, Peter Millar, Canterbury Press, 1998, ISBN 1 853112 05 4.

P105

God of work and rest – extract from *Life Together*, by Dietrich Bonhoeffer, translated by John Doberstein, SCM Press, 1954, ISBN 0 334009 04 9. In North America © 1954 Harper & Brothers, copyright renewed 1982 by Helen S. Doberstein. Reprinted by permission of HarperCollins Inc.

P108

Ordinary IV – from *A Book of Blessings*, 1987 International Committee on English in the Liturgy Inc (ICEL), 1275 K Street NW, Suite 1202, Washington, DC 20005-4907, USA.

P110

A simple meal – from the essay 'Justice is Important, but Supper is Essential', by Stanley P. Saunders, in *The Word on the Street: Performing the Scriptures in the Urban Context*, Stanley P. Saunders and Charles L. Campbell, foreword by Walter Brueggemann, 2000, Wm. B. Eerdmans Publishing Co., ISBN 0 802843 93 X.

Eastern Orthodox prayer – from *Iona: Pilgrim Guide*, Peter Millar, Canterbury Press, 1997, ISBN 1 853111 66 X.

GOD'S CREATION (P113)

P114

Opening prayer – by Joyce Carlson, from *The Dancing Sun*, Volume 6, 1995, © The United Church of Canada. Used with permission.

P115

A prayer of thanks for Creation – by Ellen Cook, quoted in 'Session One: Living with Respect', in *The Dancing Sun*, Volume 8, 1999, edited by Joyce Carlson, © The United Church of Canada. Used with permission.

P117

Our ancestors – from *Prayers, Poems, Songs and Reflections from Latin America and the Caribbean*, compiled 2002, Christian Aid.

The seventh generation – quote from *Earth Under Threat: A Christian Perspective*, by Ghillean Prance, Wild Goose Publications, 1996, ISBN 0 947988 80 7.

P119

Global garden – by Pete Anderson, *Coracle*, Issue 3/32, Citizens Of Earth.

P122

Prayers and responses – from *A Harvest Festival Service*, Christian Ecology Link.

A new green dawn – prayer from 'Maker of heaven and earth, part 2', L. David Levison, Wild Goose Reflections 1, *The Apostles' Creed: A Month of Meditaitions*, ISBN 0 947988 83 1.

P125

You bless us in the earth © Christian Aid, from *Feast for Life* materials.

P126

Closing prayer – by Joyce Carlson, from *The Dancing Sun*, Volume 6, 1995, © The United Church of Canada. Used with permission.

SEEDTIME, HARVEST, FEASTING (P129)

P130

The total bread of life – by George MacLeod, extract from *Chasing the Wild Goose: The Story of the Iona Community*, p. 94, Ronald Ferguson, Wild Goose Publications, ISBN 1 901557 00 6.

To Christ the seed – Irish traditional, words translated by Panel on Worship, from *Common Ground: A Song Book for All the Churches*, Saint Andrew Press, 1998, ISBN 0 715207 53 9.

P132

Food as power – extract from the article 'Land, Food and Power' by Ian M. Fraser, *Coracle* magazine.

P134

A prayer from Sudan – prayer used by Christian Aid from *Graces from Around the World*, compiled by Richard Bowers (see note for p15).

Life is a feast – from *Pray Now, Day 25, Nourishing, Daily Devotions with the Church of Scotland*, 1997–98, Saint Andrew Press ISBN 0 861532 32 5.

P135

If the poor didn't plant – from *Prayers, Poems, Songs and Reflections from Latin America and the Caribbean*, compiled 2002, Christian Aid.

P136

Shared by all – extract from the article 'Discerning Sufficiency, An On-going Theological Task', by Ian M. Fraser, *Coracle*, Issue No. 3/3: Having Your Cake: Christians and Money.

P137

'We thank you, God of creation' © Christian Aid, from *Feast for Life* materials.

P138

Blessing of the cheese and olives – from Greece, 2nd or 3rd century, from *Eerdman's Book of Favourite Prayers*, compiled by Veronica Zundel, Eerdman's Publishing Company, Grand Rapids, Michigan, 1983.

P139

Prayer of praise and thanksgiving; prayer of intercession – from Harvest Festival resources, the Arthur Rank Centre. 'The Arthur Rank Centre is an ecumenical partnership between the churches, the Royal Agricultural Society of England and the Rank Foundation. It is the hub of Christian concern for the wellbeing of rural people. Its programmes and projects translate that concern into effective action.'
(The Arthur Rank Centre)

P141

The earth and all its fullness – prayer (adapted) from *A Harvest Festival Service,* Christian Ecology Link.

P145

'I don't like onion' – from *Out of the Shadows: a Collection of Poems from the Fourth World,* edited by Liz Prest, ATD Fourth World, 2000, ISBN 0 950851 45 1.

P146

The earth is the Lord's – words 1991 Ramon and Sario Oliano; paraphrase by James Minchin; translation by Delebert Rice. Music: Gayom Ni Higami, a traditional Ikalahan melody; arrangement © 1991 Wild Goose Resource Group, Iona Community, from *Sent By the Lord: Songs of the World Church, Vol 2,* edited and arranged by John L. Bell, Wild Goose Publications, 1991, ISBN 0 947988 44 0.

P147

A substantial faith – from the prayer 'Bought Back from the Pawnshop of Death', by George MacLeod, in *The Whole Earth Shall Cry Glory,* Wild Goose Publications, 1985, ISBN 0 950135 19 4.

READINGS FROM THE BIBLE (P151)

P152

Psalms 8, 23, 65, 104 – selected and adapted by Frances Hawkey from *The Iona Abbey Worship Book,* Wild Goose Publications, 2001, ISBN 1 901557 50 2.

FROM DIFFERENT TRADITIONS (P155)

P156

Ramadan Kareem – from *Exile in Israel: A Personal Journey with the Palestinians*, Dr Runa Mackay, Wild Goose Publications, 1995, ISBN 0 947988 75 0.

P157

'Lord! Pitiful are we, grant us Thy favour' – from *Bahá'í Prayers*, London: Bahá'í Publishing Trust, 1975 (rev. ed.), pp89–90. Reproduced by permission of the National Spiritual Assembly of the Bahá'ís in the UK.

P158

'Jesus's countrymen lived much closer to nature than do most of us today' – from *Meaning the Lord's Prayer*, The Very Rev. Dr George Reid, Wild Goose Publications (out of print).

P159

Four Gathas – reprinted from *Present Moment Wonderful Moment: Mindfulness Verses for Daily Living*, Thich Nhat Hanh, Parallax Press, 1990, with permission of Parallax Press, Berkeley, California, www.parallax.org.

P162

'The courts are polished and decorated' – from chapter 53, *Tao Teh Ching*, Lao Tzu, in *The Complete Works of Lao Tzu*, translation and elucidation by Hua-Ching Ni, SevenStar Communications Group, Inc., 1979, 1995, ISBN 0 937064 00 9.

'The Master said' – by Confucius, from *The Analects*, Book 7 (7:16), in *Confucius: The Analects*, World Classics, translated with an introduction by Raymond Dawson, OUP, 1993, ISBN 0 192830 91 0. Reprinted by permission of Oxford University Press.

CREATOR, SON & HOLY SPIRIT (P163)

P167

A tea-time grace from Sri Lanka – from *The Ceylon Churchman*, Volume 92, no. 5, and included in Christian Aid Week materials 2003. Used by permission of Kithu Sevena, Sri Lanka.

GOD OF COMMUNITY (P171)

P173

Living in community – from *George MacLeod: A Biography*, Ronald Ferguson, Wild Goose Publications, ISBN 1 901557 53 7. Quote originally from the BBC film *Can These Stones Live?*, 1964.

P178

Who is that knocking at my door? – extract from 'Who Is That Knocking On My Door', in *I Hear hope Banging At My Back Door: Writings from Hospitality*, Ed Loring, The Open Door Community, Atlanta, with a foreword by Rev. Timothy McDonald III.

P180

A cup of rice, a cup of wheat – © 1979, Plough Publishing House. Carl Maendel, Marlys Swinger.

P185

Table prayers from the Irish tradition – from *Paidreacha na nGael (Traditional Irish Prayers)*, by Fr Vincent Madden, OCSO, Mount Melleray Abbey, Cappoquin, Co. Waterford, Ireland. Published by Melleray Press, 1975.

P186

A simple and colourful feast – by Stella Durand, from *Graces: A Collection of Table Graces for Use Before and After Meals* (see note for p15).

Thankful hearts – by Stella Durand, from *Graces: a Collection of Table Graces for Use Before and After Meals*, compiled by Stella Durand, home-produced and sold in aid of the Community of Aidan and Hilda.

P187

Du bist unser alles – the text of this song is taken from 'Du bist unser alles', edited by Paul Werner Scheele, 1989 echter-Verlag Würzburg.

P188

'Your attitude when you are eating' © Eileen Caddy – from *The Findhorn Family Cook Book* © Kay Lynne Sherman, Findhorn Publications, 1981. New revised edition, *The Findhorn Book of Vegetarian Recipes*, published by Findhorn Press, 2003. ISBN 1 84409 015 9.

'The more food your body absorbs from the garden' © Eileen Caddy – from *The Findhorn Family Cook Book*, see above.

SILENT GRACES (P195)

P196

'In silence, without rite or symbol' – from *Quaker Faith and Practice: The Book of Christian Discipline of the Yearly Meeting of the Religious Society of Friends (Quakers) in Britain*, 2nd edition, 1999, Quaker Home Service, ISBN 0 852453 07 8.

P198

'The silence sometimes observed' – from *Parable of Community*, Brother Roger of Taizé, © Ateliers et Presses de Taizé, 71250 Taizé Community, France, 1980, 1984, ISBN 0 264667 32 8. Edition translated by Emily Chisholm and the Brothers and first published in English 1980 by A.R. Mowbray & Co. Ltd, Saint Thomas House, Becket Street, Oxford, OX1 1SJ, reprinted and updated 1984.

'At table, times of silence ...' from *No Greater Love: Sources of Taizé*, Brother Roger of Taizé (A), Geoffrey Chapman Mowbray, a Cassell imprint. Originally published as *Amour de tout amour*, © Ateliers et Presses de Taizé 1990, translation Ateliers et Presses de Taizé, 1991.

ONE BODY IN YOUR NAME (P201)

P203

We praise and bless you – by Stella Durand, from *Graces: A Collection of Table Graces for Use Before and After Meals* (see note for p15).

A Malagasy saying – from *Graces: A Collection of Table Graces for Use Before and After Meals* (see note for p15).

P205

A sign of your peace – from *A Taste for Peace: Recipes and Reflections*, Pax Christi (see note for p86). Originally from CAFOD Prayerbook. CAFOD (The Catholic Agency for Overseas Development) is a major British charity that has been fighting world poverty since 1962. 'We believe that all human beings have a right to dignity and respect and that the world's resources are a gift to be shared by all men and women, whatever their race, nationality or religion.' *(CAFOD)*

P206

Spirit of Justice, Way of Love – from *Abraxas Book of Hours*, © 1983 The Congregation of Abraxas, One Lawson Road, Kensington, CA 94070, USA. 2002 reprint available (£10.00 including postage) from Richard Boeke, 16 St Mary's Gardens, Horsham RH12 1JP, UK.

Food for our souls – from the prayer 'An earth redeemed' by George MacLeod, in *The Whole Earth Shall Cry Glory*, Wild Goose Publications, 1985, ISBN 0 950135 19 4.

BODY AND SOUL (P209)

P210

Christ came in a body – by George MacLeod, extract from *Chasing the Wild Goose: the Story of the Iona Community*, p. 94, Ronald Ferguson, Wild Goose Publications, ISBN 1 901557 00 6.

'Thank you, our God, for giving us so many things richly' – by Stella Durand, from *Graces: a Collection of Table Graces for Use Before and After Meals* (see note for p15).

Ethiopian grace – adapted by Christian Aid from the liturgy of the Ethiopian Orthodox Church, from *Food for Life* harvest materials.

P211

Bless to us, O God – Celtic traditional prayer, from *The Iona Abbey Worship Book*, Wild Goose Publications, 2001, ISBN 1 901557 50 2.

P218

Gratitude – a remedy – from *A Manual of Traditional and Complementary Medicine*, ISBN 1 851582 74 6, Verlag A. Vogal, Teufer (AR), Switzerland, 1952: Mainstream Publishing, 7 Albany Street, Edinburgh EH1 3UG, 1990, reprinted 2001.

SPECIAL OCCASIONS (P235)

P236

Advent – from *A Book of Blessings*, 1987 International Committee on English in the Liturgy Inc (ICEL), 1275 K Street NW, Suite 1202, Washington, DC 20005-4907 USA.

All pilgrims need nourishment – from *Peacemaking Day By Day: Daily Readings*, Pax Christi, USA, 1996, ISBN 1 872370 05 5.

P238

Lent – from *A Book of Blessings*, 1987 International Committee on English in the Liturgy Inc (ICEL), 1275 K Street NW, Suite 1202, Washington, DC 20005-4907 USA.

P239

Lord, when you broke bread – from *A Taste for Peace: Recipes and Reflections*, Pax Christi (see note for p86).

EACH TIME WE EAT (P245)

P246

A grace in Kikongo – from *Graces from Around the World*, compiled by Richard Bowers (see note for p15).

Each time we eat – source unknown, from *Graces: A Collection of Table Graces for Use Before and After Meals* (see note for p15).

P247

Imela – from Nigeria, words traditional, music © 1990 Christ Church Gospel Band, Uwani-Engu; as taught by Mrs Unoaku Ekwegbalu; arrangement © 1990 Wild Goose Resource Group, Iona Community, from *Many & Great: Songs of the World Church Volume 1*, ed. & arr. by John L. Bell, design by Graham Maule, Wild Goose Publications, ISBN 0 947988 40 8.

P250

A simple grace in Croatian – from *Graces from Around the World*, compiled by Richard Bowers (see note for p15).

P254

Before you finish your breakfast – Martin Luther King, from *Peacemaking Day by Day: Daily Readings*, Pax Christi USA, 1996, ISBN 1 872370 05 5.

Table grace for the middle of the day – by Fritz Baltruweit, 'Tischgebet' from *Sinfonia Oecumenica: Worship with the Churches in the World,* Evangelische Missionswerk in Hamburg, Deutchsland, 1998. English translation by Jeffrey Myers.

P262

How come? – by Morag Wilkinson, from *Prayers for a Dying World: Poems with a Conscience,* self-published.

P266

Reflections on using a teaspoon, Prayer on picking up a teaspoon, Stir, Prayer relating to a fork, Fork, Knife, Prayer when drinking tea/coffee – all from the booklet *Traidcraft at Iona: Justice and Peace Prayers,* Traidcraft, 1996. 'In April 1996, in the first week after Easter, 97 Traidcraft reps, retailers, helpers and staff journeyed to Iona, the beautiful island to the SW of the Isle of Mull, western Scotland. We said we were on retreat but, because of the shared experience, renamed it an advance!

'The idea was to study and to emulate the spirituality of the Celts and discover whether there was a relevance for Traidcraft Justice and Peace people in the 1990s. Our retreat theme was 'A Mary Time for Marthas', linking the fact that Traidcraft people are do-ers of the word and sometimes we need to be listeners.

'The Celts had a prayer for virtually everything they undertook and likewise we were encouraged to commune with God in everything we saw, thought and did and through the fellowsip we shared with one another. These prayers and reflections were a gift from God to us. They were composed by the people who attended, who, in opening themselves to a God of creation, were a source of blessing to all.

'Our two main sessions were titled "work as prayer" and "prayer as work". The latter session was used to compose prayers associated with everyday objects. Everyone was given one of the following: knife, fork, spoon, mug, biro, paper, handkerchief, video, book, wire coathanger, etc. ...'

(From the introduction, *Traidcraft at Iona: Justice and Peace Prayers*)

Traidcraft is the UK's largest free trade organisation, which was set up in 1979 to challenge the unfair way in which international trading systems are usually structured. Small businesses in 'the third world' countries face many disadvantages in trade. These include: lack of money, unpredictable world prices and demands for products, tariff quotas which limit how many of their products other countries can buy, a lack of knowledge about how trading systems operate. *(Traidcraft)*

... AND FOR DESSERT (P275)

P276

Oranges for dessert – by Jean Vanier, extract from *Community and Growth*, Darton Longmann and Todd, Ltd, 1989, ISBN 0 232518 14 9.

Last summer's blueberries – by Rita Baker, story previously published in *Angles*, a parish magazine; *Surprise*, a national magazine of the United Church of Canada, 1970; In *Review*, published as an insert, with illustrations by Aba Bayefsky, Provincial Library Service, 1971; *Storytellers' Rendezvous*, Canadian stories to tell children, Canadian Library Association, 1979.

P280

Grapes – by Ruth Burgess, from *On Ground Level*, Ruth Burgess, Wild Goose Publications (out of print).

P281

The fruit (salad) of the Spirit – by Inderjit Bhogal, extract from the article 'The fruit (salad) of the Spirit', in *Flame: the Methodist magazine*, September/October 2002.

FOR THE END OF MEALS (P285)

P291

The meal enjoyed – by Stella Durand, from *Graces: A Collection of Table Graces for Use Before and After Meals* (see note for p15).

Rune of the peat fire – Celtic traditonal prayer, from *Chasing the Wild Goose: The Story of the Iona Community*, Ronald Ferguson, Wild Goose Publications, ISBN 1 901557 00 6. Celtic traditional texts of *Carmina Gadelica* were republished by Floris Books, Edinburgh, 1992.

P292

Lord, how glad we are – from *Prayers, Poems, Songs and Reflections from Latin America and the Caribbean*, compiled 2002, Christian Aid.

P292

'O most merciful Redeemer, Friend, Brother' – St Richard of Chichester, from *Praying for the Dawn: A Resource Book for the Ministry of Healing*, Ruth Burgess & Kathy

Galloway (eds), Wild Goose Publications, 2000, ISBN 1 901557 26 X.

P293

Alone with none but thee – prayer attributed to St Columba, from *Praying for the Dawn: A Resource Book for the Ministry of Healing*, Ruth Burgess & Kathy Galloway (eds), Wild Goose Publications, 2000, ISBN 1 901557 26 X.

Go forward – from *Quaker Faith and Practice: The Book of Christian Discipline of the Yearly Meeting of the Religious Society of Friends (Quakers) in Britain*, 2nd edition, 1999, Quaker Home Service, ISBN 0 852453 07 8

P294

As you have been fed – by Kate McIlhagga, from *The Pattern of Our Days*, Wild Goose Publications, 1996, ISBN 0 947988 76 9.

God of the hungry – by Jean Mortimer, reproduced from *Words for Today 1999*, edited by Maureen Edwards, with the permission of International Bible Reading Association, ISBN 0 719709 09 1.

P295

Make us worthy – from *The Iona Abbey Worship Book*, Wild Goose Publications, 2001, ISBN 1 901557 50 2.

Blessing – by Jan Sutch Pickard, from 'An Agape service', in *The Iona Abbey Worship Book*, Wild Goose Publications, 2001, ISBN 1 901557 50 2.

P296

International peace prayer – from *The Iona Abbey Worship Book*, Wild Goose Publications, 2001, ISBN 1 901557 50 2.

P297

It is not true – extract from an affirmation by Allan A. Boesak to WCC VI assembly on the theme 'Jesus Christ, the Life of the World'. In *Gathered for Life: Official Report, WCC VI Assembly, Vancouver, Canada, 1983*. Ed. David Gill, 1983 WCC Publications, WCC Geneva.

P298

'O God, you promise a world' – © Christian Aid

One world – two tables – by Erik Cramb, extract from *Parables and Patter*, Wild Goose Publications (out of print).

P300

I believe – from *Prayers, Poems, Songs and Reflections from Latin America and the Caribbean*, compiled 2002, Christian Aid.

P302

The king and the peasant – from *Peacemaking Day by Day: Daily Readings*, Pax Christi USA, 1996, ISBN 1 872370 05 5.

P303

Haleluya! Pelo Tsa Rona – from *Freedom Is Coming: Songs of Protest and Praise from South Africa*, collected and edited by Anders Nyberg, Wild Goose Publications, ISBN 0 947988 49 1.

P307

Washing up – from *Quaker Faith and Practice: The Book of Christian Discipline of the Yearly Meeting of the Religious Society of Friends (Quakers) in Britain*, 2nd edition, 1999, Quaker Home Service, ISBN 0 852453 07 8.

NOTES

1. Quotation taken from the Wresinski Report, Father Joseph Wresinski (founder of ATD Fourth World), published by ATD Fourth World.

2. This line taken from the article 'A Kairos for Scotland', John Harvey, *Coracle*, Issue No. 3/2: Sacred to the Spirit.

3. 'Jesus Christ, the poor God of Nazareth, of Pollok, of Muirhouse', taken from the article 'A Kairos for Scotland', John Harvey, *Coracle*, Issue No. 3/2: Sacred to the Spirit.

4. Quote from the article 'Land, Food and Power' by Ian M. Fraser, *Coracle* magazine.

5. A musical setting to this grace can be found in the songbook *Common Ground: A Song Book for All the Churches*, Saint Andrew Press, 1998, ISBN 0 715207 53 9.

6. 'That every minute a million pounds is spent on weapons of war, while 25 children die because of hunger' – SIPRI (Stockholm International Peace Research Institute), *2002 Yearbook: Armaments, Disarmament and International Security*, Oxford University Press, quotes world military expenditure 2001 as $839 billion. ($839 billion divided by 365/24/60 gives $1,596,271 = £1,000,000. '25 children' statistic from UNICEF).

7. Mayenziwe, a traditional South African melody, can be found in *Common Ground: A Song Book for All the Churches*, Saint Andrew Press, 1998, ISBN 0 715207 53 9.

8. 'But Jesus does not travel alone' – Ed Loring, from *I Hear Hope Banging at My Back Door: Writings from Hospitality*, The Open Door Community, Atlanta, 2000.

9. The tune Alabanza, Puerto Rico, © Pablo Fernandez Badillo, from *Sent by the Lord*, ed./arr. John L. Bell, Wild Goose Publications, 1991, p. 57, ISBN 0 947988 44 0.

10. The tune 'Compliment' can be found in the songbook *The Courage to Say No*, ed. John L. Bell & Graham Maule, Wild Goose Publications, 1996, ISBN 0 947988 78 5.

11. From the booklet *What is the Iona Community?*, Wild Goose Publications, 2000, ISBN 1 901557 32 4.

12. A variation on a grace attributed to the Very Rev. Lancelot Fleming, once Dean of Windsor.

13. Maranatha – Music: Yezu Azal: Awo, Congolese Renewal © Artemas CCN.

14. 'Our broken … beautiful lives' – by Peter Millar, from the poem 'A place of hope', in *An Iona Prayer Book*, Peter Millar, Canterbury Press, 1998, ISBN 1 853112 05 4.

CONTRIBUTORS

Dick Acworth is a father to four, a grandfather to three and chaplain to six siblings, 24 nephews and nieces and (so far) 17 great nephews and nieces.

Ewan Aitken is a Church of Scotland minister whose main source of income is now as a Labour Councillor on City of Edinburgh Council. He also writes and does a little broadcasting. He has been a member of the Iona Community since 1988.

George Amoss Jr is a Quaker (member of the Religious Society of Friends) who lives in Baltimore, Maryland, USA.

Eddie Askew is a best-selling Christian author. With his wife, Barbara, he worked in India for 15 years and later became International Director of the Leprosy Mission. His twelve books of meditations and prayers have raised more than £1.75 million for the work of the Mission. He was awarded the OBE 'for services to leprosy relief'.

Sheila E. Auld is a priest in the Church of England and recently retired after working full-time for 14 years with women on the MeadowWell Estate at the Cedarwood Trust, a pastoral care centre. During this time she led a writing group which published two books and staged performances of its work. She continues her ministry at her parish church and also as a volunteer at Cedarwood. She writes sermons, novels and poetry.

Fritz Baltruweit is part of the Centre for Worship and Church Music, Evangelical-Lutheran Church of Hannover in Hildesheim, and Consultant for Projects and Communication/PR in the regional church office in Hannover. He has served for many years with the German Evangelical Kirchentag, the Lutheran World Council and the World Council of Churches, and has published extensively (books and CDs), particularly in the areas of liturgy and music.

Ron and Rita Baker live on the shores of Georgian Bay, Canada. Ron, a former librarian, is a storyteller who specialises in bringing scriptures to life. Rita is a writer and editor. Together Ron and Rita enjoy welcoming guests to the retreats and storytelling gatherings they host at their Bruce Peninsula home, Bethany, where 'every meal is a celebration'.

John Bartholomew was ordained in 1958 by Yukon Presbytery of the Presbyterian Church, USA, to serve the Alaska Highway Parish, later earning a ThD from Princeton Theological Seminary, and chairing the sociology department at The Lindenwood

Colleges, in St. Charles, Missouri. He went on to hold posts in the southern Presbyterian Church, USA, until he retired in 1999. He has also served as a volunteer in mission with the Evangelical Presbyterian Church, Ghana, and has chaired both the Committee on the Office of the General Assembly and the Assembly Committee on Ecumenical Relations.

Jane Bentley worked for the Iona Community for nearly three years as Craft/Programme Worker at the MacLeod Centre on Iona. Before that, she was a puppeteer, and she now works and studies as a community artist in Glasgow.

Inderjit Bhogal is married to Kathy, has two children and is passionately committed to the achievement of justice for all. In the Jubilee Year 2000 he was President of the British Methodist Conference. Currently he is Director of the Urban Theology Unit, and minister with Wincobank Undenominational Chapel on the Flower Estate, Sheffield.

Camilla Björkborn is 26 years old and comes from Lulea, in the north of Sweden. She first visited South America in 1999 and felt that she left part of her heart there when she left. In 2002 she spent the year working with street-children in Cochabamba, Bolivia. She is currently spending another six months in Bolivia doing similar work.

The Rev. Dr Richard Boeke is Secretary of the World Congress of Faiths, graduate of Yale and Columbia, and received his Doctor of Ministry degree from the Pacific School of Religion, Berkeley. After serving a Unitarian church in California for 21 years, he is now minister of the Horsham Unitarian Chapel. He was the last scribe of the Congregation of Abraxas, a group which contributed to the development of life-centred liturgy for Unitarians.

Helen Boothroyd – *see Introduction and 'God of Community' section.*

Richard Bowers is a member of Bloomsbury Central Baptist Church, London. On Sundays the church provides lunch for members, friends and visitors, and for many years Richard has said Grace before this, for which purpose he has collected prayers from many visitors to Bloomsbury from around the world. Richard, who has Down's Syndrome, is active with his mother in BUild, the Baptist Union's work with people who have learning disabilities. In 1994 he attained the Duke of Edinburgh's Gold Award.

Alix Brown is a therapist working with young people and is a member of the Iona Community.

Catriona Budge grew up in Rutherglen, Scotland, and holidayed on Iona as a teenager. The island and the Abbey worship had a marked impact on her spirit. She emigrated to Aotearoa, New Zealand, as a young mother and brought up her four children in this spacious land. In the mid-1980s she was unemployed and learnt first hand about the injustices of colonisation, which had resulted in a high proportion of Maori being unemployed. Now in her retirement she is committed to creating situations where tauiwi (people who came later) can understand history in a different light and support the need for change. She is an associate member of the Iona Community.

Ruth Burgess is a member of the Iona Community who lives in the north-east of England. She is a writer of poetry and liturgy and is very fond of fireworks.

Joyce Clouston Carlson, a Canadian social worker and editor, has served as editor of *The Dancing Sun*, a cross-cultural liturgy resource published by the United Church of Canada as well as numerous other cross-cultural publications celebrating First Nation culture and tradition.

Claire Carson is a curate in the Lichfield Diocese. She is also doing research into the theological, spiritual and pastoral issues related to eating disorders.

George Casley is an associate of the Iona Community who delights in teaching Religious Studies and co-hosting meals.

David J.M. Coleman is an Iona Community member who was born in Birmingham in 1963. He spends his time with Zam Walker Coleman as parent to Taliesin and Melangell, and as minister with Barrhead United Reformed Church.

Jim Cotter is an ordained Anglican who is conducting an experiment at Llandecwyn near Harlech in North Wales to see if little-used churches can be brought alive as small pilgrim places offering quiet prayer, simple hospitality and thoughtful conversation. He also writes, and publishes as Cairns Publications. www.cottercairns.co.uk

Ian Cowie is a retired Church of Scotland minister who was the first Iona Community guide to Iona Abbey many years ago. He was most recently chaplain to the Christian Fellowship of Healing (Scotland) and is the author of *Prayers and Ideas for Healing Services* and *Jesus' Healing Works and Ours* based on his work with healing.

Erik Cramb is co-ordinator of Scottish Churches' Industrial Mission. He is a member of the Iona Community and a minister of the Church of Scotland.

da Noust are members and friends of L'Arche Edinburgh, a community welcoming adults with learning disabilities to a life shared with assistants and other members whose time is a gift. Community life is founded on welcoming weakness, in myself and the other, as a source of life. www.larche.org.uk

Ed Daub is an associate of the Iona Community, a retired Presbyterian minister who served the United Church of Christ in Japan 1951–63 as a Fraternal Worker, and Professor Emeritus of the University of Wisconsin-Madison where he initiated the programme in technical Japanese.

Robert Davidson contributed a series of landscape meditations to the Iona Community's *Coracle* magazine that were published as a series in the 2002 issues. He is managing editor of *Northwords* magazine. www.northwords.co.uk

Rt Rev Michael Hare Duke is a member of the Scottish Episcopal church and the former Bishop of St Andrews, Dunkeld and Dunblane.

Stella Durand is a member of the Community of Aidan and Hilda and is an Anglican clergywoman.

Maureen Edwards has served as a mission partner in Kenya, teaching Religious Education and writing scripts for Schools' Broadcasts. More recently she has worked with the Methodist Church in Mission Education and as an editor of the International Bible Reading Association (IBRA). Now, semi-retired, she is editor of the annual Methodist Church Handbook. She is particularly interested in how we carry out our mission in the local community, and has helped to set up a club (based in the local church) for people with mental health problems.

Ron Ferguson is a former Leader of the Iona Community. The author of several books, including a biography of George MacLeod, founder of the Iona Community, he is now a full-time writer and broadcaster.

Ian M. Fraser obtained an MA and a BD with distinction in Systematic Theology and then went into industry as a labourer-pastor as a member of the Iona Community which he joined in 1941. There followed Scottish Secretaryship of the SCM, 12 years in a dockyard parish, work helping to bring Scottish Churches' House into being, service in Geneva for the World Council of Churches and finally the role of Dean and Head of the Department of Mission in Selly Oak Colleges. He and his wife, before her death in 1987, were given a joint assignment by the British Mission Societies and Boards to contact basic ecclesial communities on every continent and assess their significance for the future of the Church.

James Fraser (1937–2003) lived in L'Arche for 22 years.

Jenni Sophia Fuchs was born in 1978 in Western Germany. She spent a large part of her childhood in Edinburgh, which she calls home, and returned there after finishing school to study Scottish Folklore at Edinburgh University. During that time, she worked as youth and children's worker at St Columba's-by-the-Castle Episcopal Church, and did various stints as children's worker for the Iona Community. She has since spent time studying and working in England, Wales and the USA to pursue a career in museum education.

Kathy Galloway is the current leader of the Iona Community.

Grant Gallup was born and educated in the Upper Peninsula of Michigan, receiving a BA at Alma College, Alma, Michigan, in 1954. After a period in the US Army as a draftee, he held various church posts, and was vicar of St Andrew's Church, Chicago, from 1961–1990. He is founder (1960) and director of Casa Ave Maria, Managua, Nicaragua. He is also a writer and posts 'Homily Grits' weekly at http://newark.rutgers.edu/~lcrew/homilygrits

Barry Graham was born in Zimbabwe and now lives as a co-worker at Loch Arthur, a Camphill community in south-west Scotland. He is a cheesemaker and is involved in administrative, social and cultural aspects of this diverse community.

Peter Graystone works for Christian Aid in their Churches Team, creating resources for worship and theological reflection to help Christians make a connection between their faith and what is happening in the developing world. Before that, fifteen years as a teacher and with Scripture Union made him a passionate advocate for the nurture of children in churches. His books include *Help! There's a Child in my Church!* and *A Church for All Ages*. He worships and serves as a Reader at Emmanuel Church, Croydon.

John Harrison is a member of the Iona Community. He has a keen interest and concern for environmental issues such as climate change, energy systems, pollution, waste, loss of biodiversity, organic growing, GMOs and real food.

David Hawkey is an associate member of the Iona Community and is married to Frances. A science technology teacher by trade, he is always learning from children and sharing the deep magic of creation. He learnt a lot about candles and creative worship as Sacristan on Iona in 2000. He is now involved with the International Centre for Reconciliation of Coventry Cathedral.

Frances Hawkey is an associate member of the Iona Community who worked as the housekeeper at Iona Abbey for a year. She and her husband David now live in Coventry where they are involved in local and world justice issues, and the work of International Reconciliation based at the Cathedral.

Alan Hawkins took his nose off the grind-wheel at fifty having worked in the electricity industry and church youth work. Since then he has travelled extensively, and lived on Iona and in Uganda. He now gives Christian hospitality in Kilmartin, Argyll, where he has a guest house.

Donald Hilton, a minister for 45 years, is the author of several books, including *Table Talk* published by the URC, and the compiler of numerous collections of worship resources, including *Liturgy of Life* and *No Empty Phrases* published by Christian Education. He is a former Moderator of the General Assembly of the United Reformed Church and was Moderator of the Yorkshire Synod of the Church for ten years.

David Jenkins is a minister of the United Reformed Church, serving in Wilmslow, Cheshire. He has also served for twelve years as Moderator of Northern Synod and is a past Moderator of the General Assembly. He has contributed prayers and meditations to numerous publications and anthologies across the denominations.

David Johnson, educated at Cambridge and Oxford, was ordained in the Church of England in 1979 and served in various parishes. He retired from full-time stipendiary ministry in 1996 and now serves part-time in the Oxford diocese.

Linda Jones is Spirituality Materials Coordinator at CAFOD, the Catholic aid agency. She is editor of *Journey to the Light* (Darton, Longman and Todd, 2003), *Turn the Tables* (CAFOD, 2003) and *Celebrating One World* (HarperCollins, 1998).

Jenny Joyce and Alan Whear have been singing together and with friends for many years, and create songs and ceremony to celebrate the festivals of the turning year. This grace was originally written for a Lammas ceremony, but has since found its way into group life as a thanksgiving song at shared meals.

Josef Kaszoni is a Unitarian minister in Budapest, Hungary, who spent a year studying in Manchester at UCM. He also writes and translates.

Mary Lou Kownacki, OSB, has lived and worked in inner-city Erie for over 30 years, and her articles on nonviolence and spirituality have appeared in numerous publications. She is executive director of the Inner City Neighborhood Art House in Erie and director of Benetvision, a publishing outreach. Her latest book is *The Nonviolent Moment* published by Pax Christi USA.

L. David Levison has been a member of the Iona Community since 1943.

Pat Livingstone is a composer and music educator based in London. Recent work includes: 'Sacrifice' for wind and string quartet, shortlisted for performance by the London Chamber Group; 'Two Steps Forward' for flexible ensemble, shortlisted by COMA for Tate Liverpool project interpreting a painting into music; 'Carmina Gadelica' – songs to be published as a CD by Wild Goose Publications; 'Move-meant' for solo cello performed by Forum London Composers' Group.

Ed Loring is a partner at the Open Door Community in Atlanta, Georgia, USA and a cofounder of the Grady Coalition, which conducts non-violent protests to help ensure affortable health care for the homeless and poor in the Atlanta area. He holds a PhD in church history from Vanderbilt University, where he specialised in American religious history, particularly churches and slavery. He and his wife, Murphy Davis, live at the Open Door. *(from* I Hear hope Banging At My Back Door*)*

Rachel McCann comes from a Merseyside mining town, but has found her home between the landscape and people of the Isle of Mull and Glasgow. The colour, trees, socialism and spirituality of both places inspire and challenge. She is currently enjoying writing, reading and doing environmental and social justice projects collectively with other women. She recently worked as co-ordinator of the Iona Community's Camas centre on Mull.

Kate McIlhagga was a minister, latterly in Northumberland, involved in writing, retreat work and the local hospice until she died in 2002. She was a member of the Iona Community and of its area of concern exploring spirituality.

Runa Mackay has worked with Palestinians since 1955 and has had, she says, 'to watch their situation getting worse and worse but I work on, in hope and with admiration for their steadfastness'.

George MacLeod, the founder of the Iona Community, was a charismatic man of prayer and action whose life spanned the 20th century. Giving up a promising career as minister to the middle classes in Edinburgh, he took up a post in the poor and depressed area of Govan in Glasgow, where he moved inexorably towards socialism and pacifism and his theology became more mystical, cosmic and political. In 1938 he initiated the venture of restoring the ancient abbey on Iona, out of which the Iona Community developed.

Ailsa Maley is a friend of the Iona Community and lives in Australia.

Joy Mead is a new member of the Iona Community. She works freelance as a poet, writer and editor and leads small creative writing groups. For many years she has been involved with justice and peace and development education groups. Poetry is her main interest and her poems have been included in many magazines and anthologies. She is author of *The One Loaf* (Wild Goose Publications, 2001) and *A Telling Place* (2002).

Rosie Miles lives in Birmingham and lectures in English at the University of Wolverhampton. She has also contributed to *Praying for the Dawn* (1999) and *A Book of Blessings* (2001), both published by Wild Goose Publications.

Peter Millar is a writer and activist and former Warden of Iona Abbey who worked for many years in the Church of South India. His latest book is *Finding Hope Again: Journeying Through Sorrow and Beyond*, Canterbury Press, 2003.

Yvonne Morland is a poet and writer with a passion for liturgical exploration. She has been writing material for Wild Goose Publications since 1995 and has been a full member of the Iona Community since August 2002. She is about to engage on a more sustained piece of writing, exploring the importance of vulnerability in human exchange, which will hopefully appear in published form towards the end of 2004.

Jean Mortimer is a retired minister of the United Reform Church in the UK and a free-lance writer of prayers and Bible study resources.

Jeffrey Myers serves as pastor, together with his wife Andrea, at the early-Gothic Alte Nikolaikirche (12th century) on the Römerberg, Frankfurt's public square. Since receiving his ThD in homilectics (practical theology) in 1996, he has developed an extensive outreach ministry to the thousand or so visitors and tourists frequenting the historic Lutheran church each day.

John Newton is currently writing up his doctorate, which examines seventeenth-century beliefs about ghosts, at St Mary's College in the University of Durham. He will shortly be looking for a job where he can put his talents to good use. He is competent at washing and ironing, having done the communal laundry when working with the Sion Community in Essex about four years ago. All reasonable offers will be considered.

Helen O'Donnell is the Iona Community's youth outreach worker.

Neil Paynter is a former member of the Iona Community's resident group on Iona. He is from Canada, and has worked in homeless shelters and nursing homes.

Jan Sutch Pickard is currently Warden of the Abbey on Iona. A member of the Iona Community, she formerly worked as an editor of Methodist publications – a desk job – whereas she now enjoys leading pilgrimages over the hills. She is, to the best of her ability, she says, a preacher, a poet and a storyteller; a bread-maker and a picker-up of crumbs. She is the editor of *Dandelions and Thistles* and co-author of *Advent Readings from Iona* (both Wild Goose Publications, 1999 & 2000).

Betty Pike is a Noongah woman from the south-west of Western Australia. Her great-grandfather was an Irish convict, and her great-grandmother was one of the Minang people of Western Australia. Betty lives in regional Victoria, is active in promoting reconciliation between Indigenous and non-Indigenous Australians, and is writer-in-residence with Aboriginal Catholic Ministry in Melbourne, Australia.

Christine Polhill is a priest in the Lichfield diocese and a member of the Iona Community. She and her husband John are creating five gardens on the Christian spiritual journey, each with an ecological theme.

Ghillean Prance was formerly Director of Kew Gardens and is now Director of the Eden Project in Cornwall. He is author of *Earth Under Threat: A Christian Perspective*, Wild Goose Publications, 1996, ISBN 0 947988 80 7.

The Very Rev. Dr George Reid was a Chaplain to the Queen. He was awarded a Doctorate of Divinity by Aberdeen University in 1972 and was moderator of the General Assembly of the Church of Scotland. He was also an associate of the Iona Community.

Bishop Patrick Rodger was born in Helensburgh in 1920 and died in 2002. A child of the Scottish Episcopal Church, he ended his ministry as the bishop of two English Dioceses in succession, Manchester 1970-78 and then Oxford 1978-86. One of the major concerns of his whole life was the unity of the Church. He was President of the European Conference of Churches and chairman of the Churches Unity Commission. As well as his commitment to Church unity, Bishop Patrick Rodger had outstanding pastoral gifts. *(The Scottish Episcopal Church)*

Victoria Rudebark is originally from Sweden but now living in Glasgow. She is a free-lance author and translator and an associate member of the Iona Community.

David Scott writes almost every day – 'It's been one of my rituals for many years.' He works as a cook, lives in a woodland and loves the sea.

Nicola Slee is a freelance theologian and writer based at the Queen's Foundation for

Ecumenical Theological Education in Birmingham. She has published poems and prayers in many anthologies, and a collection of her own work is to be published by SPCK shortly.

Graham Sparkes is a Baptist minister. Having served in two churches he now works at the central offices of the Baptist Union of Great Britain, helping churches engage with issues of social justice. He is part of 'Table Fellowship', a group that meets each week to pray and eat together.

Stephanie Tashkoff lives in Melbourne, Australia, and works with the Uniting Church in Australia's social justice office there. She is also involved with an ecumenical project, the Indigenous Hospitality House, which supports Indigenous Australians who travel to Melbourne to be with relatives in hospital. Previously Steph worked with the Middle East Council of Churches in Jerusalem, as a Uniting Church mission worker.

Fiona Ritchie Walker works for the fair trade organisation Traidcraft in the PR & Communications department. Her poetry is widely published in magazines and anthologies. She is a local preacher in the Methodist Church.

Mark Westbrook is a part-time doctor and he uses the grace he contributed to this book at home.

Alan Whear – *see under Jenny Joyce and Alan Whear.*

Kathleen White is a poet and founder member of the Association of Christian Writers. She has had ten books published by HarperCollins in the *Heroes of the Cross* series and has also written a book of children's fables.

Maire-Colette Wilkie is a 'recidivist peacenik'. A nun for thirty years, she was swept off her feet by her co-worker in the peace movement as a result of an arrest at the nuclear submarine base at Faslane. Now a member of the Iona Community, she and Alan continue to plague the Courts of Law and work hard at their joint membership of the Roman Catholic and Church of Scotland communities.

Morag Wilkinson is originally from Strathaven in Lanarkshire, but is currently working as a languages teacher in Kirkcudbright, on the Solway Coast of Scotland. She started writing poetry while at university in Stirling, and continued while working on Iona and in France, Germany and Kenya.

Jean Williams is a member of the Iona Community and runs workshops on Celtic Spirituality in both Canada and the UK.

Trevor Williams is the leader of the Corrymeela Community.

Brian Woodcock is a United Reformed Church minister in St Albans. He is a member of the Iona Community and was Warden of Iona Abbey from 1998 to 2001.

Sheila Woodcock joined the Iona Community in 1975 and was a member of the resident group on Iona from 1998 to 2001.

Sandy Yule is a minister of the Uniting Church in Australia. He was a Lecturer in Theology at Sia'atoutai Theological College, Tonga, and graduated from Princeton Theological Seminary with ThD Presently, he is 'Dean of the Theological Hall, Melbourne'.

Unfortunately it was not possible to obtain biographical details of every contributor.

INDEX OF TITLES

INDEX OF AUTHORS & CONTRIBUTORS

THE IONA COMMUNITY

The Iona Community, founded in 1938 by the Revd George MacLeod, then a parish minister in Glasgow, is an ecumenical Christian community committed to seeking new ways of living the Gospel in today's world. Initially working to restore part of the medieval abbey on Iona, the Community today remains committed to 'rebuilding the common life' through working for social and political change, striving for the renewal of the church with an ecumenical emphasis, and exploring new, more inclusive approaches to worship, all based on an integrated understanding of spirituality.

The Community now has over 240 Members, about 1500 Associate Members and around 1500 Friends. The Members – women and men from many denominations and backgrounds (lay and ordained), living throughout Britain with a few overseas – are committed to a fivefold Rule of devotional discipline, sharing and accounting for use of time and money, regular meeting, and action for justice and peace.

At the Community's three residential centres – the Abbey and the MacLeod Centre on Iona, and Camas Adventure Camp on the Ross of Mull – guests are welcomed from March to October and over Christmas. Hospitality is provided for over 110 people, along with a unique opportunity, usually through week-long programmes, to extend horizons and forge relationships through sharing an experience of the common life in worship, work, discussion and relaxation. The Community's shop on Iona, just outside the Abbey grounds, carries an attractive range of books and craft goods.

The Community's administrative headquarters are in Glasgow, which also serves as a base for its work with young people, the Wild Goose Resource Group working in the field of worship, a bi-monthly magazine, *Coracle*, and a publishing house, Wild Goose Publications.

For information on the Iona Community contact:
The Iona Community, Fourth Floor, Savoy House, 140 Sauchiehall Street,
Glasgow G2 3DH, UK. Phone: 0141 332 6343
e-mail: ionacomm@gla.iona.org.uk; web: www.iona.org.uk

For enquiries about visiting Iona, please contact:
Iona Abbey, Isle of Iona, Argyll PA76 6SN, UK. Phone: 01681 700404
e-mail: ionacomm@iona.org.uk